ANNE FRANK AND THE CHILDREN OF THE HOLOCAUST

ANNE FRANK

AND THE

CHILDREN

OF THE

HOLOCAUST

BY

CAROL ANN LEE

VIKING

VIKING
Published by Penguin Group
Penguin Group (USA) Inc., 345 Hudson Street, New York, New York 10014, U.S.A.
Penguin Group (Canada), 90 Eglinton Avenue East, Suite 700, Toronto, Ontario, Canada M4P 2Y3
(a division of Pearson Penguin Canada Inc.)
Penguin Books Ltd, 80 Strand, London WC2R 0RL, England
Penguin Ireland, 25 St Stephen's Green, Dublin 2, Ireland (a division of Penguin Books Ltd)
Penguin Group (Australia), 250 Camberwell Road, Camberwell, Victoria 3124, Australia
(a division of Pearson Australia Group Pty Ltd)
Penguin Books India Pvt Ltd, 11 Community Centre, Panchsheel Park, New Delhi – 110 017, India
Penguin Group (NZ), Cnr Airborne and Rosedale Roads, Albany, Auckland 1310, New Zealand
(a division of Pearson New Zealand Ltd)
Penguin Books (South Africa) (Pty) Ltd, 24 Sturdee Avenue, Rosebank, Johannesburg 2196, South Africa

Penguin Books Ltd, Registered Offices: 80 Strand, London WC2R 0RL, England

First published in the U.K. in 2006 by Penguin Books Ltd.
First published in the United States in 2006 by Viking,
a member of Penguin Group (USA) Inc.

1 3 5 7 9 10 8 6 4 2

Photo credits
Pages 15, 22, 61, 68, 80, 105, copyright © Anne Frank-Fonds/Anne Frank House, Amsterdam/
Hulton Archive/Getty Images; Pages 28, 53, 57, 73, 91, 119, 137, 158, 181, 194, copyright © Getty Images;
Page 87, copyright © Jacqueline van Maarsen; Page 143, copyright © the family of Hannah Senesh;
Page 203, copyright © Eva Schloss

Text permissions can be found at the back of the book.

LIBRARY OF CONGRESS CATALOGING-IN-PUBLICATION DATA
Lee, Carol Ann.
Anne Frank and the children of the Holocaust / by Carol Ann Lee.
p. cm.
ISBN 0-670-06107-7 (hardcover)
1. Frank, Anne, 1929–1945. 2. Jews—Netherlands—Amsterdam—Biography—Juvenile literature.
3. Jewish children in the Holocaust—Netherlands—Amsterdam—Biography—Juvenile literature.
4. Holocaust, Jewish (1939–1945)—Netherlands—Amsterdam—Personal narratives—Juvenile
literature. 5. Amsterdam (Netherlands)—Biography—Juvenile literature. I. Title.
DS135.N6F73388 2006
940.53'118092—dc22
2006009610

Printed in the U.S.A.
Set in Berling
Book design by Kelley McIntyre

For Linda

CONTENTS

ANNE FRANK AND THE
CHILDREN OF THE HOLOCAUST

INTRODUCTION

In September 1939, when World War II began, there were more than one and a half million Jewish children living in countries occupied, or soon to be occupied, by Hitler's armies. By 1945, when the war ended, over a million of those children—including Anne Frank—were no longer alive.

Most of them were not killed by bombing raids or in the line of duty; they were deliberately murdered by the leaders and followers of a political party that believed they had no right to live, simply because they were Jewish. Other children whose ethnic origin, religion, or parents' political choice meant that they had no place in a Nazi-led society were also targeted.

Because the Nazis were in power for so long (1933–1945), thousands of children never had a normal childhood. Something as simple as going to a local swimming pool with friends or kicking a soccer ball around a park during the summer evenings was strictly forbidden. Ordinary activities such as going to the movies were banned to them. After the war broke out in 1939, these same children faced an even more terrible future. Often torn away from their families, they were pushed into ghettos (sealed-off areas of towns where Jews were forced to live in extreme poverty) and slave-labor camps, where starvation and disease raged. Thousands more were killed by firing squads.

In the spring of 1942, mass deportations began, with trains rolling out from every occupied country taking Jews to the concentration camps in Eastern Europe. Children were sent with their families or alone to the camps, where hardly any of the very young survived; they were not able to work hard, and therefore the Nazis had no use for them. Most children under the age of fifteen were killed. Girls were less likely to survive than boys because they were seen as the weaker sex and could give birth. The Nazis wanted to ensure that Jewish life was destroyed, not created.

Despite all this, children often turned out to be braver and more capable than many adults. Being so young, they were able to adapt more quickly to certain situations. In the ghettos, for example, children smuggled food and sold anything they could find to raise money for their families. They also refused to give in to despair: They sang songs, made their own games and toys, and studied schoolbooks, even though all these things were forbidden. Like Anne Frank, many children kept diaries, using whatever paper was available to them. They wrote in office ledgers, on scraps of newspaper, and even—in the case of a young brother and sister in the Lodz ghetto—in the margins of an old French novel.

The diary of Anne Frank is the best known, and she has become a symbol of all the children who died during the Holocaust. In total, six million Jews were killed by the Nazis. Such a huge number is hard to imagine. But in the same way that we can learn more about Anne Frank's world by understanding the Holocaust, by looking in detail at her short life, we begin to understand that "six million" means six million individuals who once had hopes and dreams for the future just like us. In this way, we realize that the Holocaust isn't about impossible numbers; it's about people.

ONE:

"AS WE ARE JEWISH . . ."

Anne Frank was born in the German city of Frankfurt-am-Main on June 12, 1929. Her grandfather was a country boy who came to Frankfurt to make his fortune. He opened his own bank business in the city and married a young woman whose ancestors had lived in Frankfurt for over four hundred years. Anne's father, Otto, was born on May 12, 1889 (the same year as Adolf Hitler), and had a happy, privileged childhood. He and his two older brothers Robert and Herbert, and younger sister Leni, were brought up in a large house in Frankfurt's Westend district. Their home was filled with antiques and enormous family portraits in gilt frames. At the back was a large garden; the front overlooked an elegant square.

Anne later wrote that her father had had "a real little rich boy's upbringing, parties every week, balls, festivities, beautiful girls, waltzing, dinners, a large home, etc." A photograph of a family gathering in Germany's Black Forest in 1900 shows Otto Frank (then nine years old) in a crisp white sailor suit—the trendiest outfit for boys at that time—while Leni, Robert, and Herbert are also fashionably dressed. They all attended good schools, spoke several languages, learned how to ride, and played musical instruments. Anne loved to hear her father talk about his childhood when she was in hiding; to her it seemed like a distant fairy tale.

When Otto Frank was eighteen, he began studying economics at Heidelberg University. There he met Nathan Straus, whose family owned Macy's department store in New York. Nathan and Otto quickly became good friends, and when Nathan went back to America, he invited Otto to join him there, working in Macy's, which was then the world's biggest department store. Otto eagerly accepted, juggling his time at Macy's with another job at a New York bank. Then one day Otto received a telegram telling him that his father had died, and he returned to Germany. He found a new job with an engineering company in Dusseldorf and was still working there when World War I broke out in 1914.

Although the Franks were Jewish, they did not have much interest in their religion. Otto rarely attended synagogue and didn't read or speak Hebrew, the ancient Jewish language. The district where the Franks lived was popular with many Jewish families and had a synagogue at its center, but Otto was brought up to take more pride in his German roots than in his religion. Not long after the war began, he and his brothers joined the German army, and his mother and sister worked in hospitals, taking care of wounded German soldiers.

Otto was by now in his twenties, a natural leader who was friendly and fair with everyone he met. He was made an officer, and then a lieutenant, and proved himself a brave soldier on the Somme and at Cambrai, two of the worst battles in history. He was certain that his country would win the war, but in 1918 Germany surrendered and Otto returned to Frankfurt.

The Franks' bank business had lost a great deal of money during the war. Otto tried to improve the situation by opening a branch of the bank in Amsterdam, where business was better than it was in Germany. Unfortunately, it wasn't a success, and once more he went back to Frankfurt. By now, Otto was thirty-six years old. He had been engaged when he was nineteen, but it hadn't worked out, and now he was eager to marry and have children.

He met Edith Hollander, then twenty-five, and found that despite her shyness, she was kind and intelligent and shared his interest in art, literature, and family life. She was also a modern young woman who loved fine clothes, dancing, music, and vacations with her large circle of relatives and friends. She was one of four children; her sister Betti had died of appendicitis at the age of sixteen, but

Edith was close to her two older brothers, Julius and Walter, who had also served in the German army. Like Otto's, her childhood, in the German city of Aachen (close to the Dutch border), had been happy and secure. Her father was a successful businessman who had made a lot of money dealing in scrap metal. Edith was more religious than Otto; her family attended synagogue regularly and kept a kosher household, observing the Jewish dietary laws.

Otto and Edith married on May 12, 1925, in the synagogue in Aachen where the Hollanders were lifelong members of the congregation. After a honeymoon in Italy, the couple returned to Frankfurt, where they lived with Otto's mother for two years.

Both Otto and Edith looked forward to being parents and were overjoyed when their first child, Margot Betti, was born on February 16, 1926. A peaceful baby who slept through the night almost from birth, with a shock of dark hair and big, wondering eyes, Margot was her mother and father's "little angel." She grew into a quiet, well-behaved child, eager to please everyone and with a sunny outlook on life. She was eighteen months old when her parents decided they needed a place of their own. They found a large apartment to rent on Marbachweg, in an unfashionable part of Frankfurt. The apartment was on two floors of a huge house, with a balcony overlooking the houses behind theirs. Margot had her own bedroom next door to her parents' room, and there was also a room for their housekeeper, Kathi, a cheerful young woman whom Margot adored.

As the months passed and Margot became a toddler, she made friends with a girl named Hilde, who lived in one of the other apartments, and with Gertrud, a slightly older girl who lived in the house next door. Hilde and Gertrud were Catholics, and Mr. and Mrs. Frank encouraged Margot to take an interest in her friends' religion, which she did, playing "church" with Hilde in her apartment and attending Hilde's Communion party.

There were other children living on the bottom floor of the house, but neither Margot nor Hilde nor Gertrud played with them: Their father was the landlord and a keen supporter of the Nazi Party. His children never tried to make friends with Margot, Hilde, or Gertrud. They had probably been forbidden to play with Margot, for by this time a tidal wave of hatred against the Jews was sweeping through Germany and would one day engulf all of Europe.

The Franks' landlord was just one of several thousand supporters of the growing Nazi Party. The Nazis promised a bright future for Germany and singled out Jews as the root of the country's problems, which had begun with the end of the war in 1918. The countries that had won the war—including Britain, France, and the United States—put together the Versailles Treaty in 1919. This was basically a list of rules that Germany had to obey as punishment for starting the war. Under the treaty, Germany had to give up some of its land and pay for the damage—a colossal sum—caused by the war. The German army and navy also had to be cut back, and the entire political structure of Germany had to be altered according to the new rules. These demands deeply angered many Germans, who felt humiliated by the treaty.

All this had a disastrous effect on the German economy, causing inflation and unemployment to soar. Nonetheless, a new Germany arose called the Weimar Republic, more democratic than before, and based on an elected parliament, the Reichstag. Among those committed to rebuilding Germany were many Jews. But there was someone else, too, who wanted to make Germany great again, someone who saw the opportunity to grasp power and create a nation unlike any other in Europe.

His name was Adolf Hitler.

Born in a small Austrian town in 1889, Hitler had fought in the German army in the war and won the Iron Cross for bravery. He had always dreamed of becoming an artist, but when the war ended with Germany's defeat, he decided to go into politics instead. When the National Socialist German Workers' Party (NSDAP or Nazi Party) was created in 1920, Hitler immediately became a member and saw himself as future leader of the party. He hoped to lead the Nazis to victory in the German parliament and set out a program for them to follow.

Among Hitler's policies for the party was the rule that "None but members of the Nation may be citizens of the State. None but those of German blood, whatever their creed, may be members of the Nation. No Jew, therefore, can be a member of the Nation." He demanded that Jews who had entered Germany after 1914 should be expelled from the country, and when he addressed a crowd in a Munich beer hall in August 1920, his theme was "Why We Are Against the Jews." He talked of a "thorough solution" to ridding Germany of its Jews.

For a while, it seemed that Hitler would fail in his political ambitions. He was jailed after trying to seize power from the existing government. Most of his time in prison was spent writing his anti-Semitic book *Mein Kampf* ("My Struggle"), which expressed his deep hatred for Jews. But when he was released from prison, he quickly became leader (*Führer*) of the Nazi Party.

In 1929, the New York stock market crashed, causing a worldwide depression and making the economic crisis in Germany even worse. Hitler knew that people wanted someone to blame and were looking for a way out of their problems. He offered them both, holding the German government and the Jews responsible for the country's misfortunes. He told voters that if they supported him,

Germany would become the most powerful nation on earth. He said that he would ignore the terms of the Versailles Treaty and that the German people were not responsible for the high levels of unemployment and widespread poverty. Hitler pointed his finger at the Jews, calling them dishonest, money-grabbing, and dangerous. He branded them "race polluters" and spoke of the "pure" blood of non-Jewish Germans. According to Hitler, as members of the "Aryan race," Germans were the most advanced people on earth.

These ideas appealed to many Germans who listened to Hitler, spellbound. They wanted to regain their pride in themselves and their country. They had grown up with the idea that Jews were different. The clothes and religious beliefs of Orthodox Jews seemed sinister to them, and many Germans associated Jews with the Communist Party, a political party whose members believed that everyone should contribute to society according to their abilities and receive according to their needs. Jealousy was also an issue: Despite everything, Jewish people had worked hard to rise to the top of several professions and had built strong communities. They had a sense of identity that many non-Jewish Germans felt they lacked. Jews were the focus of Hitler's rage, although he also spoke out against black people, Roma and Sinti—or "gypsies"—the mentally and physically handicapped, and homosexuals. To an enthusiastic Germany, Hitler declared that none of these groups could ever be part of the Aryan Master Race.

It was into this terrifying world that Anne Frank was born, in 1929.

It was seven thirty in the morning, on June 12, 1929, when Annelies Marie Frank was born in Frankfurt's city hospital. Her birth had been long and difficult, and the nurses were so tired they accidentally wrote in the hospital register that the eight-and-one-quarter-pound baby was "a male child"! Within a few hours of her birth, Anne had had her first photograph taken by her proud father, and was given a necklace with a Hebrew inscription on one side, and her birth date and the words "Lucky Charm, Frankfurt" on the other. Mrs. Frank kept baby books for both her daughters, and in the one for Anne, she wrote: "Mother and Margot visit the baby sister on June 14. Margot is completely delighted. Home on June 24. At night for six weeks she cries a lot. Julius and Walter [Anne's uncles from Aachen] arrive by car on July 6. Anne is suffering from the heat wave."

The baby's first smile, when she was just a month old, was for her father. Anne soon became a real daddy's girl, while Margot favored her mother more. Mr. Frank was a good father and, unusually for that time—when men didn't generally play a very active role in their children's early lives—he played with his daughters, bathed them, fed them, changed their diapers, and told them stories before they went to sleep each night. Mrs. Frank took care of her children during the day, but when Mr. Frank came home from work, he liked to spend as much time with them as possible.

In August of 1929, the family traveled to Aachen for a holiday with Mrs. Frank's family, and little Anne cried all the way. In Aachen, she settled down, and Mrs. Frank wrote in the baby book that Anne was happy if someone, especially her uncle Julius, came into her room in the mornings. Mrs. Frank added, "Anne does so many silly things. We return home on September 3. Anne sleeps all the way." These baby books tell us how different Anne and Margot were as children. Margot was always very quiet, well behaved, and neat (Kathi called her "the little princess"), while Anne slept badly, cried a lot, and was often quite disobedient. This pattern continued as the two of them grew older. Mr. and Mrs. Frank always held Margot up as an example to Anne, who found this very frustrating and annoying. When they were very young, Margot and Anne were both popular girls who loved fun and games, although Anne liked to get into mischief. One morning, when Anne was a toddler, Kathi found her sitting on the balcony in the rain, in the middle of a puddle. She was giggling, and even when Kathi picked her up and scolded her, she didn't cry, but asked if Kathi would tell her a story—while she, Anne, went back to her puddle!

Anne (center) and Margot with Otto Frank, August 1931.

Anne liked to have her own way and said things that she really shouldn't. But she was such a lively, affectionate, and friendly girl that no one could be cross with her for long—especially not her father, who was always the one who managed to get her to sleep at night by telling her the stories his mother had told him when he was young, about two sisters, Good Paula and Bad Paula. Anne loved these tales and later wrote one of her own, when she was in hiding. Her story was about Bad Paula during the First World War and how she accidentally found herself in a plane headed for the enemy territory of Russia. Eventually Paula found her way back to Germany, where she was happy to be with her family again.

Despite their different characters, Margot and Anne played together often, and with Hilde and Gertrud, too. Gertrud liked to babysit Anne, feed her, and change her diapers. The girls played in Hilde's backyard, where there was a sandbox and a swing. Anne and Margot were also frequent visitors at the house of their paternal grandmother (Omi) in the west end of the city. Omi could be very firm and had the air of a queen when she walked, but she was so kind that the girls loved her deeply, and liked to cuddle up with her in bed when they stayed at her house. Omi was a real storyteller and wrote poetry, too. Every week, she would tell Margot and Anne about a group of mice that had adventures. Anne was always happy to listen to these stories. She was quickly growing into an observant, talkative little girl who liked to make people laugh and to be the center of attention. Omi called her "little woman" and said she had an old head on young shoulders.

Margot and Anne's bright, chatty aunt Leni (Mr. Frank's sister) also lived in Omi's house with her husband and two young sons, Stephan and Buddy. Both boys loved to play tricks and pranks. When Anne was older, she and Buddy found that they shared a sense of humor and loved dressing up, but when Anne was still very small, Buddy and Stephan liked to push Anne around the neighborhood in her baby carriage. One day out almost ended in disaster. Buddy remembers: "My brother and I took Anne in her pram outside. We went racing around and around the street but we couldn't get the curb right and the carriage tipped up. Anne flew out of the pram! We told no one, of course, and Anne was okay."

Anne and Margot also looked forward to visits from their maternal grandmother (Oma) in Aachen and their uncles Julius and Walter. Oma Hollander was very calm and quiet, and took a great interest in everything Margot and Anne said and did. She was angelic, like Margot, and Mr. and Mrs. Frank sometimes asked her not to be too soft with the children, especially Anne, who was very strong-willed. Julius and Walter had no children of their own and enjoyed spoiling the girls. Anne and Margot loved their uncles, and because their father didn't own a car, they were always excited when Uncle Julius or Uncle Walter offered to take them out in his car.

These early years in Frankfurt, so happy and carefree for Anne and Margot, were coming to an end. Their housekeeper, Kathi, who would soon be leaving them to get married and set up a home of her own, appeared one day looking troubled. When Mr. Frank asked her what was wrong, she told him that she had spoken to the washerwoman, who said she had been unable to sleep the night before because of fighting in the streets caused by Brownshirts. Kathi asked Mr. Frank who the Brownshirts were. Mr. Frank, fully aware that the Brownshirts were anti-Semitic Nazi thugs who attacked Jews at any opportunity, tried to make a joke out of it so that his children wouldn't become alarmed. But Mrs. Frank said in a serious, quiet voice, "We'll find out soon enough who they are, Kathi."

The real name of the Brownshirts was the SA. They were Hitler's bodyguards, but their duties included attacking Jews and political opponents. The brown uniforms they wore led to their being known as "Brownshirts" by everyone in the country. With the SA roaming the streets, Jews were no longer safe; there were assaults on Jews in cafés, theaters, shops, and synagogues. Bystanders either watched curiously or walked away. Few dared to try and stop the violence.

As more people joined the Nazi Party, enormous parades and rallies were held, which in turn drew voters, just as Hitler had hoped. At these rallies, often held in the evening, and by torchlight, thousands of Nazis in their distinctive uniforms marched together, holding the red party flag with its black swastika (an ancient religious symbol) in a white circle. They pledged to support Hitler, chanting *"Heil Hitler"* and thrusting out their right arms in the Nazi salute to their leader.

The parades and rallies were the most spectacular political events Germany had ever seen. Among those watching was Otto Treumann, a Jewish boy of fourteen: "The media were completely in thrall to the Nazi Party. It took hold of you, whether you liked it or not. It was so nationalistic. . . . [F]eeling 'German' and identifying with the Fatherland were extremely appealing, now that the country was scrambling to its feet after the defeat of 1918. Scary? Absolutely! Especially when you knew that you were Jewish and that all the problems were being blamed on you."

Hitler knew that such displays would make an impression on young Germans, whose loyalty was important to his future in politics. He formed the *Hitler-Jugend* (Hitler Youth) for children between the ages of fourteen and eighteen, who were then expected to join the Nazi Party when they turned eighteen.

In September of 1930, the Nazis won 107 seats in the

Reichstag, making them the second largest political party in the country. When the new Nazi members of parliament arrived at the Reichstag that month, crowds of Hitler Youth stood outside to cheer them in. Holding the Nazi flag high, and with their hands raised in the Hitler salute, thousands of boys and girls joined the older party members in chanting, "Germany awake! Death to Jews!"

The Frank family were forced to leave their home on Marbachweg in 1931, when their landlord told them that he no longer wanted Jews living in his property. Mr. and Mrs. Frank had already thought about moving anyway, since in their part of the city, groups of Brownshirts often marched by, singing vicious songs about Jews. The Franks found a new home on Ganghoferstrasse, in a quieter, prettier part of Frankfurt with fields nearby. Most of their neighbors were doctors and lawyers, and there were some Jewish families among the Christian ones. Nazi soldiers didn't march around on the streets of this suburb, and the house itself was nicer, with a garden and a sandbox in the yard. Margot and Anne made new friends quickly, and saw their old friends, too.

When summer came, Mrs. Frank filled an old bathtub with water so that Anne and Margot could play in it on hot days. Anne was not allowed out of the garden alone, and her favorite spot was the sandpit, where she could play all day if Margot was out with older friends. In the winter, when it snowed, the fields nearby were perfect for tobogganing, and Anne loved being pulled around on a sled by Margot, or having snowball fights. They still played with their cousins, Stephan and Buddy, and looked forward to vacations in Aachen with their mother's family, who often visited them in Frankfurt as well.

In the spring of 1932, Margot started school. It was quite close to home, and no one cared that she was one of the few Jewish girls in her class. She was well liked by everyone and proved herself to be a smart girl who worked very hard in her classes. But she was never the nerd Anne later teased her about being; she liked to be with her friends and play games or go bicycling as well. She was still a quiet, polite girl, and always would be. Anne was learning to talk very well, and sometimes said things that embarrassed people. She was only a toddler when she and Oma got onto a busy streetcar and no one gave them a seat, prompting Anne to pipe up: "Won't anyone stand up for this old lady?" Whatever popped into Anne's head quickly popped out of her mouth.

While their father was working, Anne and Margot's mother would often take them into the town center of Frankfurt. There were many stores and lots of pleasant little cafés where Mrs. Frank sometimes arranged to meet her friends. Anne and Margot were happy to let her chat while they ate delicious cakes. Both girls were always as

Edith Frank with Anne (left) and Margot in Frankfurt, 1933.

well dressed as their mother, who liked to buy clothes for her children as much as for herself. One photograph taken of them around this time shows Margot in a very chic outfit of shiny shoes, knee socks, a skirt, a sharp jacket, and a hat, and Anne in a fluffy white coat. They would usually visit one of the big department stores in town before going home in time to greet Mr. Frank returning from work.

After their evening meal and bath, Mr. Frank read to his daughters or made up stories for them, just as he always had. Both girls loved when their father spent time with them, and they gave him a special name: Pim. Mr. Frank was still an avid photographer and took many pictures of Margot and Anne playing, reading, or simply sitting together. They were exceptionally pretty little girls, with large, long-lashed eyes and the same thick, dark brown hair as their mother.

Although their home life was happy, Nazism had gained a firm grip on the city of Frankfurt. Mr. Frank tried to joke about the Nazis to his wife and children, but other friends and relatives remember that he was seriously worried about the future. Violence against Jews was growing more and more common, and the streets of Frankfurt were full of cruel graffiti about Jews. Some Jewish-owned stores had their windows defaced by slogans in white paint, and the Nazi flag hung from many houses, stores, and offices. The swastika was everywhere: on stamps, posters, even cups and plates. Every day, groups of Nazis marched through the streets looking to cause trouble for the Jewish citizens of the city.

On January 30, 1933, Mr. and Mrs. Frank were visiting friends and listening to the radio when it was announced that Hitler had been appointed Chancellor of Germany. Their host said cheerfully, "Well, let's see what the man [Hitler] can do!" Mr. Frank later recalled, "I could not reply, and my wife sat as if turned to stone."

The Nazi Party had gained enough votes in the elections to give them the majority in the Reichstag. Germany was now under Nazi rule.

TWO:

"WE EMIGRATED TO HOLLAND . . ."

By 1933, it wasn't only the Nazis who were giving Mr. Frank cause for concern. The bank business was failing, and his income was much lower than before. Anne's omi asked if they would prefer to give up their apartment and live with her, which would save them quite a bit of money, so at the end of March of 1933, they moved in with Omi. Her house must have seemed huge to them after their apartments, and the girls had an even bigger garden to play in than before, although they were farther away from their friends and Margot's school. She began attending a new school nearby, but it was very different from her old one. This time, because she was Jewish, Margot had to sit apart from her "Aryan" classmates with the other Jewish children. Her parents were deeply unhappy about it and so was Margot; she liked to get along with everyone, and had never suffered discrimination until then.

The segregation of Jewish and non-Jewish children at Margot's school led to Mr. and Mrs. Frank's decision to leave Germany. The year before, they had discussed emigrating. Mr. Frank recalled, "As early as 1932, groups of Brownshirts came marching by singing, 'When Jewish blood splatters off the knife.' This made it more than clear to everyone. I immediately discussed it with my wife: 'How can we leave here?' but then there is also the question, 'How will you be able to support yourself if you go away and give up more or less everything?'" Other family members had recently left Germany to begin new lives elsewhere. Anne and Margot's cousins, Buddy and Stephan, had moved with their parents to Switzerland, where their father was manager of Opekta, a company selling pectin, a gelling ingredient used in jam making and other kinds of food production. Otto Frank's brother Herbert had emigrated to Paris, and his other brother, Robert, was living in London with his wife, where they had opened an antiques business.

Mr. Frank considered living with one of the other family members abroad, but he also needed a job of his own. His brother-in-law in Switzerland suggested that he open up a branch of Opekta in Amsterdam, Holland. Mr. Frank liked the idea; it would get them all out of Germany to a place where he already had friends and which he knew quite well. He decided this was the best answer to their problems, and in June of 1933, he traveled by train from Frankfurt to Amsterdam.

Anne and Margot stayed behind with their mother in Omi's house until their belongings could be sent on to Aachen, where they would live with Oma Hollander, Uncle Walter, and Uncle Julius until their father found them a home in Amsterdam. When they left Frankfurt, Omi closed up the house where she had lived for thirty years and took a train to Switzerland, where she moved in with her daughter's family.

After that, there were no members of the Frank family living in Frankfurt anymore. Hitler was beginning to achieve his aim of making life in Germany so difficult for Jews that they had no option but to leave.

With the setting up of the Hitler Youth, Hitler had begun to turn his attention to Germany's youth and children. He banned all youth groups except those approved by the Nazi Party and made clear his ambitions: "A youth will grow up before which the world will shrink back. A violently active, dominating, intrepid, brutal youth. Youth must be all those things. It must be indifferent to pain. There must be no weakness or tenderness in it. . . . With that I can create the new order."

Boys between the ages of six and fourteen were pressed into joining the *Jungvolk Deutsches* (German Young People), while those aged fourteen to eighteen were guided toward the Hitler Youth. There were two groups for girls: the *Jung-*

A Hitler Youth parade in Nuremburg, Germany, 1938.

madel (Young Girls), for girls between the ages of ten and fourteen, and the *Bund Deutscher Mädel* (League of German Girls) for those aged fourteen to eighteen. Thousands of boys and girls willingly joined, attracted by the sporting and camping activities promised by the Nazi Party. Their leaders told them that they were superior to everyone else and that they were needed to fight a battle of "good versus evil" against Jews. Girls were not led to expect a career; they were taught that motherhood—providing new blood for the Nazi state—should be their greatest aim and were given lessons in housekeeping and child care.

At the same time, Hitler stepped up his campaign against Jews. One month after gaining power, the Nazi Minister of Propaganda, Joseph Goebbels, announced a nationwide boycott of Jewish-owned stores, Jewish doctors, and Jewish lawyers. News of this reached Britain and America, and in New York, some people protested against the planned boycott by asking everyone not to buy German goods.

Their actions made little impression on the Nazis. At ten o'clock on the morning of April 1, 1933, in villages, towns, and cities throughout Germany, groups of Brownshirts headed toward stores, doctor's offices, and law practices owned by Jews. They painted abusive graffiti on doors and smashed windows with heavy clubs. Armed with revolvers, they stood outside the places they had attacked, warning people not to enter. A young Jewish boy named Gerard Durlacher, who later grew up to be a famous writer, watched the boycott of his grandmother's store: "Huge men in the brown uniform of the Storm-troopers are positioned on either side of the doorway with their revolvers strapped to their belts and their legs encased in shiny black boots. They are standing as still as statues. Beside them, mounted on poles, are large plac-ards with words I can understand even though I can't read. Rowdy boys, heads taller than I am, shout the slo-gans, while the adults in their musty, worn-out clothes mutter their approval or nod their heads in agreement. 'Don't buy from Jews, they will be your downfall!' and 'Jews are ruining the nation. Germans, put a stop to this now!' Stars of David have been scrawled on the broad store windows. . . ."

The boycott shocked many people, even those who had voted for Hitler. Most did not join in as the Nazis had hoped, but walked away quietly. A few deliberately entered Jewish stores to show their disapproval and to let Jewish people know that not all Germans were admirers of Hitler. The Brownshirts grabbed these people on their way out and put a stamp on their faces that read: "We, traitors, bought at Jewish stores."

On April 7, the Nazis passed a law banning Jews, black people, and other ethnic minorities from working at state schools. Hundreds of teachers were dismissed and replaced by Nazis. Hans Massaquoi, who was seven years old when Hitler became Chancellor, found that the new teachers were cruel to him because he was black. Many of them were openly rude to him and made offensive remarks about black people. Once, when Hans was about ten years old, a teacher took him outside the classroom and said, "When we've settled the score with the Jews, you'll be next."

Now all Jewish children attending schools with non-Jews were forced to sit apart from their classmates. They were humiliated and ridiculed by the teachers, who gave lessons reading from the new Nazi-regulation textbooks. One teaching manual showed a boy drawing a "Jewish" face on a blackboard above a caption that read, "The Jewish nose is bent, it looks like the number 6." Another booklet, with the title "Victory of Arms, Victory of Children," had a photograph of a German family next to a Roma (gypsy) family and informed the reader, "These are children of your own blood, and these belong to an alien race."

New lessons were introduced: Race, Genetics, and Nation. Jewish children were brought to the front of the room and used as "life objects." In the small town where she lived, Clara Wachter Feldman was singled out by her teacher: "Our class was given a new teacher, a Nazi Party member. The first day he came in, he said, 'I understand we have a Jew pig in our classroom.' Then he said, 'Now we will see how much pain a Jew pig can endure.' He had me put out my hand and he hit me with a stick." At break times, children were encouraged to play the latest board game, "Jews Out!" Jewish children lived in an increasingly isolated world, ignored by their old friends and bullied by their classmates.

The April boycott had been the first in a series of many anti-Jewish laws passed in 1933. Jewish civil servants were fired, and Jewish companies were taken over by Nazis. New war memorials excluded the names of Jewish soldiers who had died for their country. Towns and villages without a Jewish population displayed banners at their entrances proudly telling visitors that the place was "Jew-free." Jews were forced out of public life, banned from their jobs and all leisure activities. Anyone who tried to resist was either imprisoned or executed.

On May 10, 1933, in cities and towns throughout Germany, books written by Jews, homosexuals, and other forbidden authors were set on fire. In Berlin, 20,000 books were burned in front of the Berlin Opera House. From an open car parked nearby, Joseph Goebbels watched the flames from the bonfire leaping high into the night sky, surrounded by cheering Nazis. He was glad to see the books being torn apart and thrown into the fire, for he believed them to be nothing but "intellectual filth."

Two months later, on July 14, the Nazis declared a law to prevent "genetically unfit offspring" from being born. The new ruling targeted mentally and physically handicapped people, epileptics, the blind, and the deaf. They were taken to hospitals and forcibly sterilized so that they could never have children. The Nazis believed that anyone who was handicapped was a drain on the state, and that money spent caring for them was wasted. At least 400,000 people were sterilized under this new law.

Among them was sixteen-year-old Franziska Schwarz. Franziska was born deaf; her parents were hard of hearing, but her brother and several other relatives had normal hearing. Franziska and her mother were ordered to report to a hospital for sterilization. The family appealed the decision, and Franziska's mother was told that she didn't have to have the operation, but her daughter did. Franziska recalls: "I screamed all the way to the hospital. The nurse locked me in a room with two other deaf teenagers. The three of us cried all night. When the nurse came to give us tranquilizers, I tried to fight her off. She held me down and gave me the injection. In the morning, I woke up in a room full of beds. My stomach hurt. I touched the bandages and started to cry. The nurse who brought me water was crying too. 'I'm sorry, there's nothing I could do to help you. With Hitler, you have to be quiet.' Her finger pointed to the portrait of Hitler hanging over the bed. She tapped her temple with her finger, to indicate, 'He's crazy.'"

Sixty-three thousand Jews left Germany in 1933, some finding refuge in lands they had never seen, such as

Venezuela, Bolivia, Japan, and South Africa. The Jews who stayed in Germany did so hoping desperately that things would improve. Many were too old, too poor, or too sick to leave, and most people found it difficult to get away under any circumstances. Those who emigrated had to leave behind their way of life, their language, their culture, their relatives, and their friends. Not all countries welcomed Jews, and as the number of refugees grew, escape routes began to close down as Britain, the United States, Holland, and France—among several others—set limits on how many refugees they were willing to take in.

Margot and Anne didn't attend school in Aachen. Anne was still too young, and there was little point in finding a school for Margot since they hoped to be living in Amsterdam by the end of the year. Mrs. Frank wrote to the girls' friend Gertrud to let her know that they were happy in Aachen but were looking forward to living together as a family again. Mr. Frank had found temporary accommodations in Amsterdam and had opened a branch of Opekta in the city center. He spent his free time in search of a suitable apartment for his family. Mrs. Frank joined him on the weekends, leaving Anne and Margot safely in the care of Oma Hollander and uncles Julius and Walter.

At last they found an apartment at 37 Merwedeplein,

in south Amsterdam's River Quarter, a busy area popular with refugees from Nazi Germany. The suburb was still being built, and the square in front of the Franks' new home was a flat green space with trees that were only young shoots, leaving the children of the neighborhood with a small field on which to play games. All the apartments were identical, made of brown brick with large white-framed windows and orange roofs. The Franks' apartment was on the third floor, with the living-room window overlooking the square, and a gravel-covered balcony in the back that Anne called "the terrace" that was big enough to fit a couple of sunbathers. There were several stores in the area, lots of little cafés and bakeries set up by families fleeing Germany, and a real sense of community.

At the end of 1933, Margot arrived by car with her uncles Julius and Walter. Anne stayed in Aachen with Oma Hollander until February of 1934 to give her parents a chance to organize everything and to allow Margot to get used to her new school. Four-year-old Anne arrived on Margot's birthday and later wrote in her diary that she was placed on the table as a surprise present for her older sister.

The family soon settled into their new home. Mr. Frank's business was doing well. He had hired a young woman in her twenties, Miep Santrouschitz, as his secretary, and she became a personal friend of the whole Frank family. Although Miep was born in Austria, she had lived in Amsterdam since she was eleven years old and considered herself Dutch. She hated the Nazi Party, as did Victor Kugler, who worked for Mr. Frank as a manager. He was Austrian, like Miep, but had also lived in Holland for several years and was married to a Dutch woman. He became friendly with Mrs. Frank, Margot, and Anne, too, for they often visited Mr. Frank at his office on a busy street just behind the Dam, Amsterdam's main square.

Margot loved her new school on Jekerstraat, just a five-minute walk from home. She made new friends quickly and must have been very glad not to have to sit apart from any of the pupils because she was Jewish. Anne went to the neighborhood Montessori school, and during her morning walk there she often met up with her teacher, Mr. van Gelder, who lived nearby. Although Anne was so young, she was as chatty with adults as with children her own age. She always told Mr. van Gelder the latest story or poem she had made up with her father, whom she still adored.

At the Montessori school, Anne befriended Hanneli Goslar and Sanne Ledermann, who had also recently arrived with their families from Germany. Sanne lived two streets away from Anne, while Hanneli (known also as Hanne or Lies) lived on the ground floor at 31 Merwedeplein. The three girls spent a lot of time together, and Anne later wrote in her diary that "people always said, 'There they go: Anne, Hanne and Sanne.'" Lies remembers that when her mother brought her to school on her first day, Mrs. Goslar was anxious about her meek daughter and how she would react to a new school. But as soon as Lies and her mother entered the building, they saw Anne, standing opposite the main doors, happily ringing the bells to call the pupils to class. Lies forgot about her shyness and rushed over to Anne, who was equally pleased to see her.

Although Margot and Anne arrived in Holland not knowing a word of Dutch, they soon picked up the language at school. At home, they spoke a mixture of German and Dutch, but with their school friends and teachers, they only spoke Dutch. Mr. Frank understood the language very well, but Mrs. Frank, who was a housewife and didn't meet as many Dutch people as her husband and children did, found it more difficult. She missed her friends and family in Germany and her old way of life there.

Margot and Anne didn't have such feelings; they were at school with friends through the day, and in the evenings and on weekends, there was plenty to keep them occupied. Almost all the children in the neighborhood knew one another, and they met up to play hopscotch and ball games and do handstands and other tricks after school. Anne was hopeless at handstands, but joined in anyway. When her friend, a neighbor called Toosje, tried to comfort her by pointing out that she was shorter and younger than everyone else, Anne disagreed, saying, "That's still no reason not to be able to do a handstand." The girls all kept poetry albums, in which they wrote little poems about their friends and decorated the pages with cut-out pictures. During vacations and on weekends, friends called for one another by whistling a particular tune through the mail slot. To her great disappointment, Anne could not whistle, so she sang instead—five notes up, five notes down.

For the Frank family, most of the summer of 1934 was spent visiting Aachen and taking day trips to Zandvoort, a popular seaside resort not far from Amsterdam. Mrs. Frank sent a postcard to Kathi in Germany, telling her that the children were having fun and that Anne was turning into a little comedian. Things were also going well for Mr. Frank. His business was making a good profit, and the Opekta company moved to new offices on the Singel Canal, near the colorful flower market.

For the time being at least, in Holland they were safe.

In Germany, Hitler's influence continued to grow. The Nazis used propaganda as a weapon and promoted their ideas about Jews through mass rallies, radio broadcasts, and newspaper reports. One of these ideas was that Jews were working together to take over the world and rob people of their money. The Nazis often discussed a leaflet called "The Protocols of the Elders of Zion," an old piece of Russian propaganda whose writer claimed to have uncovered plans by Jews to take over the world. Although in 1937 a Swiss court declared "The Protocols" to be fabricated, the Nazis continued using it to turn people against Jews.

Spiteful untruths about Jews were published in *Der Sturmer* ("The Attacker"), the official magazine of the Nazi Party. Readers were told that Jews killed Christian children, then used their blood to make the special bread eaten at Passover, a Jewish holiday. Such stories, outrageous though they were, further set Jews apart from the rest of German society. There was no escape from propaganda; even beer mats bore the words "Whoever buys from Jews is a traitor."

The state offered no protection for those hated by the Nazis. The *Geheime Staatspolizei*, or Secret State Police, known as the Gestapo, had the power to arrest, question, and jail any German. The Gestapo, though technically police officers, allowed and encouraged terror as a means of maintaining control of the state and its citizens. There were also the black-uniformed *Schutzstaffel*, or Defense Guard, known as the SS, who served as Hitler's personal bodyguards and became an army within an army. There were many branches of the SS, and they would ultimately be in charge of the concentration camps. In addition to the SS, there were the SD, the intelligence and security branch of the Nazi Party, and the brown-shirted SA.

On September 15, 1935, two laws were passed that would affect the future of all Jews living in Europe. The so-called Nuremberg Laws were brought in "to protect German blood and German honor." The first law stated that German citizenship could belong only to "a national of German or kindred blood." The second stated that no Jew could claim to be of German blood. The laws forbade marriage and sexual intercourse between Jews and non-Jews.

The passing of these two laws helped seal the fate of six million Jews.

THREE:

"WHEN WE WERE STILL IN NORMAL LIFE . . ."

In her diary, Anne referred to her school years as "ordinary life." Despite the troubles in Germany and elsewhere, in Holland, Anne and Margot could still enjoy their childhood. Omi, Uncle Herbert, and cousin Stephan came to stay occasionally, and the Franks frequently visited them in Switzerland. Schoolwork was a slight problem for Anne, as Mrs. Frank wrote to Kathi: "Anne is not as well behaved as Margot and does not like to buckle down to things. . . ." In another letter, Mrs. Frank wrote: "Our big girl, Margot, is very hardworking and already thinks of going on to college. Little Anne is somewhat less industrious, but very droll . . . witty and amusing."

Both Anne and Margot missed some of their schooling because of sickness during 1935 and 1936. Margot suffered badly from stomachaches, and Anne had a weak heart. Anne's arms and legs sometimes dislocated, which didn't hurt her at all; sometimes she would do it on purpose so she could laugh at her friends' horrified faces. Mr. Frank recalled later, "Anne wasn't a strong girl. There was a particular time when she was growing quickly, and she had to rest every afternoon because of her health problems. She wasn't allowed to do any demanding sport, but had lessons in rhythmic gymnastics, which she loved. Then later, she learned to ice-skate with great enthusiasm. . . . Of course, she also had a bicycle, like everyone else in Holland, but she only used it to go to school, not for trips out. She preferred to stay in town than to be out in the country, and she wasn't interested at all in the trips we took around Amsterdam. She enjoyed going to the beach where she could play with other children." Anne loved to swim and won two medals at the public swimming pool in Amsterdam.

After school and on weekends, Anne spent most of her time with Lies (Hanne) Goslar. The Goslars were very religious and invited the Franks to share their Friday night Sabbath meal with them each week. The two families also celebrated the Jewish New Year and Passover together. On Wednesday afternoons and Sunday mornings, Lies studied Hebrew. Margot also took Hebrew classes, but Anne preferred to spend Sundays with her father at his office. When Lies had finished her lessons, she went along, too, and they got into mischief, calling each other on the office telephones and pretending to be secretaries. Their favorite trick, especially at Anne's apartment, was throwing buckets of cold water from the high windows onto passersby!

When Lies was asked later to describe Anne, she said honestly, "At the time of our childhood she really was a girl like other girls her age, only her development was much quicker and [later] her writing very mature." She remembers how Anne loved little secrets, and that she loved to chat. Anne collected pictures of movie stars, which didn't interest Lies, but they both began a collection of photographs of the children of the royal families of Holland and England, and would swap any doubles they had. Lies liked the fact that Anne was always ready to play jokes on people, too, and saw that she liked feeling important, perhaps because Margot was always held up as an example to her. Mrs. Goslar, who liked Anne very much, used to say, "God knows everything, but Anne knows everything better!"

Anne and Lies were inseparable. They confided their secrets, teased each other, shared the same dentist, called for each other with their special tune, and even, in 1936, caught measles from each other. Lies was sick from December 6 and Anne from December 10. They spoke every day on the telephone, but weren't allowed to meet until they were fully recovered. On December 18, Anne felt well enough to send her grandmother in Switzerland a short letter: "Dear Omi, I wish you all the best on your birthday. How are Stephan and Bernd [her cousin Buddy's real name]? Thank Aunt Leni for the beautiful ski gloves. Did you get some nice presents? Please write back. Kiss, Anne."

Two frequent visitors to the Franks' home were Mr. Frank's secretary Miep and her boyfriend Jan Gies. Jan also lived in the River Quarter and, like Miep, he wasn't Jewish, but he was as disgusted by events in Germany as she was. He worked for the social services. On their first evening at the Franks' flat, Miep enjoyed the welcoming atmosphere and noticed a charcoal sketch of a mother cat and her kittens. "The Franks were cat lovers," she noted, and saw, too, that "everywhere were signs that children dominated the house: drawings, playthings." The two girls ran in from their bedroom before dinner. Margot, at ten years old, was a beautiful child. She had the same hairstyle as her sister, and wore similar clothes, but looked much neater than seven-year-old Anne, who was talkative and confident.

Anne's large circle of friends now included a number of boys. Lies remembers, "Boys really liked her. And she always liked it a lot when all the boys paid attention to her. . . . Everyone generally liked her, and she was always the center of attention at our parties. She was also the center of attention at school." Otto noticed the same thing; Anne was becoming "a great talker and fond of nice clothes."

The Franks stayed in close contact with their relatives abroad. There were always birthday cards, letters, and little notes, although Anne's cousin Buddy can't remember Anne's gift for writing showing up in any of those: "I had no idea she could *write*! I mean, I had seen her letters and so forth but she could write letters and there was nothing special in it. I never dreamed that the lively girl who visited us on holidays had the depth Anne developed [in hiding]. Margot was the serious one, always reading books and marking crossword puzzles. She was very different to Anne. I had very little contact with Margot. Not that I didn't like her, I liked her very much, but she was no fun, very quiet." Buddy looked forward to his cousins' visits to Switzerland because he and Anne were such good friends. "I adored her because she was such a good sport—always ready for fun and games. We used to dress up and play film stars. Anne had a very keen sense of fairness and justice. Whenever we got dressed up and acted out our scenes, Anne never took the best garments for herself. She always gave them to me, and the funnier I looked, the better she liked it."

From 1936, all "Aryan" Germans over the age of ten were drafted into the Hitler Youth. Each child was given a dagger bearing the words "Blood and Honor," and learned to sing a song about making Germany great again and getting rid of the Jews. It was written by Horst Wessel, a Nazi who was killed in a street fight with Communists in 1930, and it became a second national anthem for Germany. All members of the Hitler Youth were taught how to use a gun; when the war began, many of them joined the German army and fought for their country.

Girls also joined the German army. Elisabeth Hödl was very young when she began active service. She remembers: "With the motto, 'You are nothing, your nation is everything,' an ardent patriotism was instilled in us. . . . Neither I nor my girlfriends were interested in politics. We didn't even take the trouble to read Hitler's book *Mein Kampf*. . . . We had been brought up never to criticize or express our own opinion. At school, at home, and at work, only orders and obedience to those orders existed. We didn't realize that we were quietly and gradually being molded to an inner readiness for war." Elisabeth eventually became involved in the peace movement.

Hitler was preparing for war. On March 12, 1938, German troops marched into Austria. They were welcomed by crowds of enthusiastic Nazi supporters in the capital city of Vienna. The anti-Jewish laws in Germany were brought into effect, and thousands of Austrian Jews lost everything they owned: their businesses, their homes, and their freedom. They were made to scrub the streets and clean toilets while the rest of the population and jeering Nazis looked on.

Angela Carpos, a young Jewish girl living with her mother in Vienna, recalls: "The Nazis were burning books and they came and snatched out of my hand my one and only lovely teddy bear and burnt it in front of me. They didn't hit us—but what really terrified me were the scrubbings that went on. I saw neighbors and friends being humiliated, scrubbing windows and scrubbing streets. Absolute fear ran through everybody. . . ."

Within a year, German troops entered western Czechoslovakia and its capital, Prague. Přemysl Pitter, a Czech Protestant writer who had opened a school for poor children in Prague, hid Jewish children in his school. When the Gestapo questioned him, he denied that the children were Jewish. Pitter and his assistant, Olga Fierz, then brought the children secretly to a home in the village of Myto. Together, Pitter and Fierz saved one hundred Jews during the German occupation.

The situation for Jews in the occupied countries was desperate, and many wanted to get out while they could. But they were not given much help. In July of 1938, representatives from a number of countries met to discuss how many Jews they were willing to take in. All the countries wanted to keep the number of refugees as low as possible, claiming that giving shelter to Jews might give rise to anti-Semitism. This refusal to help the Jews led to millions of Jewish families becoming trapped when the Nazis closed the borders of the countries they occupied.

It was up to individuals like Varian Fry to offer them a lifeline. Fry worked for the American Emergency Committee, a private American relief organization, and he and his coworkers in Marseilles issued exit documents for Jews who wanted to leave France. After a year, Fry was fired from his job, but his actions had saved thousands, including the philosopher Hannah Arendt and artists Marc Chagall and Max Ernst.

Life for Jews was unbearable in the occupied territories. In November of 1938, Jewish children were banned from attending school with Aryans and were sent to "Jews-only" schools. Mariella Milano-Piperno, a young Jewish girl, was appalled by the news that she was not allowed to return to school. She was ashamed, and hated telling her classmates that she wouldn't be going to school with them anymore because she was Jewish. "Why?" she wondered. "What did I do not to be allowed to go to school?"

Black children and Sinti and Roma children were also thrown out of the German education system. Hundreds of them were taken away by the Nazis to be sterilized. Hannes Weiss was a nine-year-old boy at the time. He recalls: "People would yell, 'Black gypsy, dirty gypsy.' Terrible! Then the doctors came. I was just a child. They examined us, studied how you walked, measured everything, just so that they could determine what a gypsy was. We didn't know what it was all about. Later on we did. . . ."

Among the other groups targeted by the Nazis were Jehovah's Witnesses. Elizabeth Kusserow's parents were arrested when they wouldn't give up their faith. Eventually, both her parents were released, but thirteen-year-old Elizabeth and her younger brothers got into trouble at school: "Every day the teacher reprimanded me for not saluting the Nazi flag. The big black swastika on the red banner flew over the schoolhouse and hung on a pole in every classroom. My stomach churned as I tried to think how I could avoid saluting it or saying 'Heil Hitler.' My parents had taught me to salute only Jehovah God. To salute a flag or a person was the same as worshipping idols. I wouldn't sing the horrible Nazi songs either. I kept my lips together." The headmaster sent Elizabeth and her brothers away to a reform school without telling their parents. Elizabeth's mother managed to find out where they were and convinced the principal to release them. But on the day Elizabeth and her brothers were due to leave, SS men arrived and took all three children to a Nazi training school. They remained there for six years, and were young adults by the time they saw their parents again, after the war.

During 1938, Miep and Jan often discussed politics over dinner at the Franks' apartment in Amsterdam. They all shared an intense hatred of the Nazi Party. Miep's Austrian passport had been confiscated and replaced by a German one. Mr. Frank said that it was a madness that would pass, but his wife disagreed; Mrs. Frank was extremely worried about the future. But all talk of politics stilled whenever Anne and Margot came into the room. They seemed to be growing up very quickly. Miep noticed that Anne always had bright color in her cheeks from excitement, and never spoke slowly, but always in a rush. Margot was becoming a really pretty girl who had a very quiet manner and always sat very straight and correct in company, with her hands folded in her lap. She was getting excellent grades in school. Anne's studies were improving, too, and she was turning into a social butterfly. Miep admired how neat both girls looked—Anne's untidiness was a thing of the past now, and they often wore freshly ironed print dresses with hand-embroidered white linen collars. Both girls had immaculate hair, cut in the same dark, shiny bob. After dinner, Anne and Margot went into their bedroom to finish their homework before Otto joined them for his evening storytelling session.

In March of 1938, the Franks "made the Viermerentocht" (a tour of the lakes), and after the vacation, Mr. Frank set up a second company at the offices on the Singel Canal where Opekta was located. His new business, Pectacon, was listed in the Amsterdam telephone directory as a "wholesale herb merchant, manufacturer of pickling salt and mixed spices." Mr. Frank took on a new staff member to work as an adviser for Pectacon, Hermann van Pels. Mr. van Pels had recently arrived from Osnabruck in Germany with his wife Auguste and son Peter, who was the same age as Margot. Mr. and Mrs. van Pels were both hot-tempered, cheerful people, while their son was quiet and shy. They bought a flat on the busy street behind where the Franks lived, and the two families became good friends. The van Pelses usually attended the Franks' Saturday afternoon gatherings aimed at bringing German Jews together, to help them and introduce them to Dutch people interested in their welfare.

Among the other guests was a man named Fritz Pfeffer, a Jewish dentist from Berlin, and his girlfriend Charlotta Kaletta. Pfeffer was a very cultured man who loved sports. He had been married and was now divorced. His young son lived in London, and Pfeffer missed him greatly. Another new addition to the Franks' circle was an eighteen-year-old Dutch girl named Bep Voskuijl. She worked as a typist for Mr. Frank. Tall and bespectacled, Bep was kind-hearted and painfully shy, but got along very well with the Frank family and everyone at Pectacon. No one had any idea then just how closely entwined all their lives would become.

In 1938, Mr. Frank took his daughters to Switzerland. Buddy remembers: "Our grandmother was living in an apartment because there wasn't enough room for her with us then. And the last time Anne was there, I remember we played at my grandmother's house with my puppet

theater. We took it in turns. Then we went to my grandmother's wardrobe and got dressed up. With hats and
everything! We imitated the grown-ups—we had an awful
lot of fun. We laughed ourselves sick, I remember that.
She had such a sense of comedy."

It was the last time Buddy ever saw Anne and Margot.

In October of 1938, Hitler gave orders for 15,000 Polish
Jews living in Germany to be turned out of the country.
Their homes and possessions became Nazi property. The
Polish government eventually agreed to take them in, but
many were beaten and killed by the Nazis. One of the
deportees wrote to tell his son, who was living as a stu-
dent in Paris, about their treatment. After receiving his
father's letter, Hirsch Grynszpan walked to the German
Embassy in Paris and shot the first official he saw, Third
Secretary Ernst vom Rath.

Hitler used the assassination to launch widespread
attacks on Jews in Germany, Austria, and the occupied
part of Czechoslovakia. During November 9 and 10 of
1938, 7,000 Jewish businesses were ruined, 191 synagogues burned, 91 Jews killed, and 30,000 Jewish men
deported to concentration camps. In Berlin, 8,000 Jews
were made homeless. Nazis raided synagogues for Torah
scrolls and sacred books to burn on huge bonfires lit in
the middle of Jewish neighborhoods.

The ruins of the Tielshafer Synagogue in Berlin,
burned by the Nazis in November of 1938.

Fourteen-year-old Ester Friedman witnessed the attacks in Vienna from the window of her home. "The atmosphere up and down the street was electric; we did not know why but a feeling of fear pervaded the air. I stood by the window . . . then it happened: a crowd of brown-clad SA men, with the fearful swastika armband on their sleeves, marched down the road. I leaned out further. They entered the old people's home of the Jewish community. The windows opened and out flew books. The doors opened and out came the old people, being pushed and pulled by their beards as they could not walk quickly enough for the hordes of brown-shirted youths. . . . They were made to watch their precious prayer books burn. And I watched. Buckets were brought and the ashes had to be shovelled by the old men and women. The youths and the crowds laughed at the sight. Water was brought and brushes and rags, and the old people were made to kneel and scrub the pavement. Beards were pulled until blood flowed, old women fainted—or died—I don't know. And I saw. And I smelled smoke. I turned my head and looked up the road. Our synagogue was burning—bright and high the flames roared—but I heard no fire engines."

The events became known as *Kristallnacht* (Crystal Night) because of all the shattered glass lying on pavements in front of Jewish-owned stores. A fine of one billion German marks was placed on the Jews of Germany for "provoking" the attack. The world's press reported what had happened, and the trade boycott on German goods was stepped up, but without effect. Jewish businesses were sold to Aryan retailers, and Jews were banned from yet more public places. Panic reigned in Germany as people frantically tried to get out of the country. Some 250,000 (about half the total Jewish population) had emigrated to other lands by then, including places as distant as Shanghai, China.

Kristallnacht marked a turning point in the chain of events leading up to the Holocaust. After that, it was clear to everyone, Jewish and non-Jewish, in Germany and elsewhere, that the Nazis would stop at nothing in their efforts to make Germany "Jew-free." As a result, the British government decided to take in 10,000 Jewish children. Every Western country had been asked by Jewish communities to give homes to as many children as possible, but only Britain responded. Children accepted on the *Kindertransports* (Children's Transports) had to be between ages three and seventeen, and were expected to emigrate alone, without their parents. No usual visa entry was necessary, but a document of identity and a bond of fifty pounds per child was required. The young refugees would travel through Germany and Holland in sealed trains before being put on the boat to Britain. The first group of refugees arrived in Harwich on December 2, 1938.

Dorothy Sim, a young girl living in Hamburg, practiced her English before she left. "All I succeeded in learning was 'I want to go to the WC' . . . and 'I have a handker-chief in my pocket.' Among my clothes they packed a box full of precious family photographs, my own set of cut-lery and a toilet case with cloth and soap. My father had taken the toilet case with him when he fought in the First World War. He had won the Iron Cross. I recall arriv-ing at the railway station in Hamburg. There were two stone lions guarding the entrance. I was carrying my toy dog Droll and I had my leather shoulder bag on. I dropped Droll underneath a train and a man had to climb down and rescue him. I had a peach and a pear in my shoulder bag. We children boarded the train to get our places. Then I was sent off again to say farewell to my mother and father. I can see them to this day. They were standing in a corridor behind a barrier. I said my good-byes and then walked back up the long corridor away from them and into the train."

The children were eventually either taken in by foster families, orphanages, or group centers, or sent to work on farms. Those children who had homes to go to in Eng-land, with relatives, friends, or sponsors, went straight to London, arriving at Liverpool Street Station, where they were then met by the people who would be looking after them. Most were well treated, although a few were made to work for their hosts.

Following Hitler's invasion of the rest of Czechoslo-vakia on March 15, 1939, a number of Czechoslovakian

Some of the 10,000 Jewish and non-Aryan child refugees
of the Kindertransport arriving in England, December 2, 1938.

Jewish children were also sent to start a new life in Britain. The Nazi government at first refused to allow the transports. An extraordinary Dutch woman named Gertrud Wijsmuller, who was already organizing transports of refugees, managed to get them to change their minds. She took a train to Vienna to speak to Adolf Eichmann (the Nazi official in charge of Jewish emigration), and incredibly, she persuaded him to release six hundred Austrian Jewish children. She then helped organize forty-nine other refugee transports to Britain.

The last Kindertransport left on May 14, 1940, when the war meant that no more trains could pass through Holland. Only 20 percent of Kindertransport children were reunited with their parents after the war.

In March of 1939, Anne's oma, her grandmother Rosa Hollander, arrived from Germany to share the apartment on Merwedeplein. Anne's uncles, Julius and Walter Hollander, had lost the family business to the Nazis, who "Aryanized" it by giving it to someone who was not Jewish. After Kristallnacht, Julius and Walter were arrested. Julius was freed because he had been wounded while serving the German army during the Great War, but Walter was imprisoned in Sachsenhausen concentration camp, not far from Berlin. He was sent from there to a Dutch refugee camp, and after Julius was able to prove that they had the means to emigrate, Walter was released, and the two of them fled to America.

Their mother, meanwhile, was happy in Amsterdam. Anne was ill with flu when Oma arrived, bringing with her a special gift for her youngest granddaughter. It was a beautiful fountain pen, wrapped in cotton wool in a red leather case. It later became Anne's favorite pen for writing in her diary. Oma Hollander was seventy-three, but she and Anne were good friends; she could always spare time to listen to Anne's stories about school.

Mr. Frank had to go abroad on business in May of 1939 and, knowing how much Anne missed him when he was away, he sent her a letter, which she kept "to serve as a support to me all my life." In it, he reminded her: "I have often told you that you must educate yourself. We have agreed the 'controls' with each other and you yourself are doing a great deal to swallow the 'buts.' And yet you like to spoil yourself and like even more to be spoiled by others. All that isn't bad, if deep in your heart you remain as lovable as you have always been. I have told you that as a child I, too, often rushed into things without thinking twice and made many mistakes. But the main thing is to reflect a little bit and then to find one's way back to the right path. You are not obstinate and so, after a few tears, the laughter is soon back again." Anne later wrote about the letter in her diary (where she kept it in between the pages of the book): "Jacque [a school friend] thought this was a declaration of love by some boy and I didn't try to enlighten her."

In the summer, Anne, Margot, Mrs. Frank, and Oma Hollander went on several day trips to the beach. Anne had a severe cold, but insisted on going swimming. Her tenth birthday that year was celebrated with a special party to mark her entry into double figures. She invited her favorite girlfriends. A photograph taken by her father that day shows them all standing in the sun on the Merwedeplein, linking arms and wearing their best dresses. Anne gave a copy of the picture to her best friend Lies, having written on the back: "Anne Frank's birthday party, [6-12-39]."

The scramble to leave Germany was almost over, as the Nazis began to close off all avenues of escape. On May 13, 1939, 930 desperate refugees left the German port of Hamburg on the ocean liner *St. Louis*, hoping that the U.S. government would allow them into the country. Of those on board, 734 had valid entry numbers (each refugee was given a number and placed on a waiting list), but these did not permit entry for another three years.

The ship reached the Caribbean, where the refugees appealed to Latin American countries to let them in. Twenty-four refugees were taken in by Cuba, but Colombia, Chile, Paraguay, and Argentina responded with a firm "no." The ship sailed on to Miami, where it docked for four

Anne's tenth birthday (she is second from left), 1939.

days, waiting for a reply from the U.S. government to the refugees' request to land. The government rejected their plea. The *St. Louis* was forced to sail back to Europe.

In Belgium, scores of journalists were waiting to broadcast the story of those on board the ship. The attention resulted in Britain, France, and Holland offering to take them in. Gisela Knepel, on board the *St. Louis* with her mother and sister, gained entry to Britain, where they began work almost immediately. She recalls: "Life was hard. All you were allowed to do was housework. At fifteen I was just scrubbing floors for a living. But I was happy to do it. We were happy to be saved." Gisela was one of the lucky ones: Those refugees taken in by France and Holland had only one year of freedom ahead of them before the Nazi forces invaded, trapping them again. Of the 930 refugees who had set sail on the *St. Louis*, 660 were killed in the Holocaust.

On January 30, 1939, Hitler gave a speech in Berlin in which he warned that if Germany went to war, the outcome would be "the destruction of the Jewish race in Europe." That same year, Hitler brought in the "euthanasia" project, which was aimed not at Jews, but at the mentally and physically handicapped. "Euthanasia" actually means mercy killing, and by giving the project this name, the Nazis were implying publicly that they were killing these people out of compassion, when in fact nothing could have been further from the truth. The Nazi state had always judged the impaired as "unworthy of life" and had nicknamed them "the useless eaters." By 1939, Hitler had decided on a solution: murder.

Nazi doctors registered all children born with disabilities, then told their parents that the children were being taken away to receive special medical attention. Most fathers were away in the German army, and those mothers who didn't believe the doctors and tried to rescue their children were sent to work camps. Once the children were in the hands of the Nazi doctors, they were killed with lethal injections and overdoses of medicine.

The first murders of mentally and physically handicapped children (and also adults) took place in October of 1939, in special hospital wards. The bodies of over 10,000 victims were burned in the crematorium of a mental institution in Hadamar. Church leaders protested against the killings, and in 1941, the project was officially called off. In reality, it went on, and it is thought that about 72,000 people were murdered in the euthanasia project, among them approximately 5,000 children. The actual number is probably far higher.

The killings of the mentally and physically handicapped were the beginning of the end, the precursor to the Holocaust that was about to take place. On September 1, 1939, Germany invaded Poland. Two days later, the Second World War began.

FOUR:

"GOOD TIMES RAPIDLY FLED . . ."

The first Jews to suffer during the war were the three million Jews living in Poland when Hitler's armies invaded. Approximately 350,000 Jews had homes in Warsaw, Poland's capital city, and another 202,220 lived in Lodz. The rest lived in Poland's other cities, towns, and remote villages. Until the invasion, Polish Jews had a rich cultural life with their own schools, hospitals, theaters, kosher restaurants, fine old synagogues, and a strong sense of community.

All that came to an end on September 1, when German forces launched a *Blitzkrieg* (lightning attack) on land and by air, and German warships targeted the Polish Baltic Coast. One month before, Hitler and the Russian leader Josef Stalin had agreed that after the invasion they would "share" Poland. Following the defeat of the courageous Polish army, and despite the declaration of war by Britain (who had promised to come to Poland's aid), Hitler and Stalin did indeed split the country in two. German troops entered Warsaw on September 30. Russia took control of the neighboring states of Estonia, Latvia, and Lithuania. Most of the 1,250,000 Jews living in areas ruled by the Russian government survived the war, despite being imprisoned in Soviet labor camps.

Jews living in German-controlled Poland had a very different fate. They were immediately singled out for public humiliation. Nazi soldiers cut off the beards of Orthodox Jews, forced them to perform demeaning tasks, and assaulted them in the streets. Arek Hersh, then eleven years old, lived in the Polish town of Sieradz. "I saw German soldiers dragging Jewish men from their houses, and kicking and beating them in the street; with horror I noticed that my father was among them. The Jewish men were forced to run toward the marketplace, whereupon two rows of armed German soldiers were waiting for them. They then had to run through the German gauntlet where they were savagely kicked and clubbed with rifle butts. My cousin, Idle Natal, only twenty-one years old, was kicked to death."

Horrific as all this was, it was just the beginning.

Mr. Frank's cousin Milly, who lived in London, later recalled: "During the first months of the war, Otto was virtually our only link to the Continent. We couldn't write to relations in Germany for England was at war with Germany. But Otto could write to Germany because he was doing so from neutral Holland. I got a letter from him saying how terribly unhappy he was because he was sure that Germany was going to attack. He said, 'I don't know what to do about the children. I can't talk to Edith about it. There's no use worrying her before she has to be worried. Forgive me, but I just had to write it.'" Milly suggested that they send Margot and Anne to her in England. Mr. Frank wrote back: "Edith and I discussed your letter. We both feel we simply can't do it. We couldn't bear to part with the girls. They mean too much to us. But if it's any comfort, you are the people we would have trusted."

Anne's last full year at the Montessori primary school was 1940. From the first year to the fourth, her teacher had been Mr. van Gelder. Toward the end, he noticed that Anne had a new ambition. "It is correct that she wanted to be a writer. That I remember. It started early with her, very early . . . and I imagine she might very well have become one." Anne's interest in writing came in useful during her last year at the Montessori school, when plays were performed. She had lots of ideas for scripts, but she also enjoyed performing. Despite being smaller than most of her classmates, she had no shyness and liked imitating people. Her teacher at the time was the headmistress, Mrs. Kuperus. She remembered Anne vividly. "Anne was a lovely girl, not conspicuous, but always active and spontaneous. . . . She was intelligent, but I had more intelligent children in the class. I do know that she loved reading and drama too, she reveled in drama."

In his memoir written many years after the war, Anne's father looked back on his younger daughter's first school years: "She hated maths. I practiced her times tables with her countless times. She only did well in those subjects that interested her, particularly history. One day she came to me and said that she had to give a short speech to the class about Emperor Nero. 'Everyone knows what's in the history books about him, what else is there for me to say?' To help her, I took her with me to a friend of mine who had a large library. There she got some specialist books, which she took home with pride. A while later I asked her about her speech. 'Oh,' she said, 'my classmates didn't want to believe what I told them because it was so different from what they knew about Nero.' 'And what about the teacher?' I asked. 'He was very pleased,' she answered."

In the spring of 1940, Anne and Margot began writing to two pen pals in America. The exchange was arranged by Birdie Matthews, a young teacher from Iowa who had recently visited a friend of hers (also a schoolteacher) in Amsterdam and brought home a list of Dutch children wanting pen pals. She asked her pupils to pick out names from the list. Juanita Wagner, who lived on a farm in Dan-

Anne on the flat roof of her house at Merwedeplein, 1940.

ville, chose Anne Frank. In her letter, she told Anne about her home life, her family, and her older sister Betty Ann, who also wanted a pen pal. Anne wrote back immediately, enclosing a postcard, photos, and a letter from Margot for Betty Ann. The letters were written in English; Mr. Frank probably translated them from Anne and Margot's originals in Dutch. Anne's letter to Juanita read:

Amsterdam, 29 April, Monday.

Dear Juanita,

I did receive your letter and want to answer you as quick as possible. Margot and myself are the only children in our house. Our grandma is living with us. My father has an office and mother is busy at home. I live not far from school and I am sitting in the fifth class. We have no hour classes we may do what we prefer, of course we must get to a certain goal. Your mother will certainly know this system, it is called Montessori. We have little work at home.

On the map I looked again and found the name Burlington. I did ask a girl friend of mine if she would like to communicate with one of your friends. She wants to do it with a girl about my age not with a boy.

I shall write her address underneath. Did you yourself write the letter I received from you or did your mother do it? I include a post-card from Amsterdam and shall continue to do that collecting picture-cards, I have already about 800. A child I used to be at school with went to New York and she did writh [sic] a letter to our class some time ago. In case you and Betty get a photo do send a copy as I am curious to know how you look. My birthday is 12th of June. Kindly let me know yours. Perhaps one of your friends wil [sic] write first to my girl friend, for she also cannot write English but her father or mother will translate the letter.

Hoping to hear from you I remain
Your Dutch friend
Annelies Marie Frank.

P.S. Please write me the address of a girl. The address of my friend is [Sanne's address follows].

Juanita, Anne's pen pal, recalls: "Needless to say, we were both thrilled to have established communications with a foreign friend, and we both wrote again imme- diately. However, we never heard from Anne or Margot again. . . . We assumed their letters could not get through because of censorship." Juanita's sister Betty Ann continues: "We often talked and wondered about the family. Did they have enough food? Were the bombs dropping nearby? . . . To be very honest, we grew up in a small country town. There were some Jewish people there but it was no big deal. It never dawned on me that the other girls were Jewish. If we had known, we would have prayed and done more."

On September 21, 1939, at a secret meeting in Berlin, SS General Reinhard Heydrich, Chief of the Reich Security Main Office, spoke with a number of leaders of SS groups in Poland. He kept his plans for Polish Jews secret, but told the SS men that he wanted vast areas of western Poland cleared of Jews, and those Jews living in large towns and cities were to be confined to certain districts or "ghettos." Wherever possible, the ghettos—surrounded by high brick walls and barbed wire, and patrolled by armed guards—would be in cities where the railway connections were good. This was a deliberate move, ensuring that the next stage of the Nazis' plan—which was yet to be unveiled—would be far easier.

Ghettos sprang up throughout Poland. Samuel Pisar was twelve when he and all the other Jews in his home city of Bialystok were ordered into a ghetto. After the announcement, Samuel's family gathered in the living room of their home, still in shock. Samuel remembers that it was a hot summer day, but a fire roared in the fireplace and into it his father threw the family's most cherished possessions, such as photographs, letters, and heirlooms. "We are living," he said, "our last moments in our home. We don't know when we will return. We don't know who will move in here after we have gone. Each of us is allowed to carry one bag. That means the barest essentials, only what will keep us alive. Everything else must be left behind."

Samuel protested: "But father, what about my bicycle? And my ice skates? And my stamp collection? And my—"

"Bicycles are not allowed. Your ice skates will be useless. As for your stamp collection, take it along. We may be able to trade it for food. But that's all."

The largest Polish ghetto was in Warsaw. Forty thousand Jews lived there, crowded and miserable. There was no privacy: Families had to share one room with several strangers. Sewage was everywhere and starvation was rife. Children walked the streets all day, hunting for food. An eyewitness remembers: "There are always heaps and piles of filth on the pavements. Often a child will snatch a packet from a passerby and run away, ravenous over the food inside. Even when he is caught and beaten, the young creature will not give up his meal. . . . There are always countless children inside the ghetto. People on the Aryan side gape curiously at the pitiful spectacle presented by these tattered gangs. In fact, these gangs of children are the

Jewish children on a tram in Warsaw's ghetto, circa 1940.

ghetto breadwinners. If the German looks away for one second, they run nimbly over to the Aryan side. The bread, potatoes and other things that they buy there are hidden under their rags, and then they have to slip back the way they came."

The second largest ghetto in Poland was in Lodz. Conditions were no better there, but most children still wanted to play games, to read, and to learn. They had nothing, so they invented their own games. One of these involved empty cigarette packets. The children removed the bright tops of the packets and piled them up until they had enough to make a whole deck of cards. They played with them as if they were the real thing, shuffling them, dealing them out, and arranging them by color and name. They thought up their own games and played for hours.

Several children in the Lodz ghetto are known to have kept diaries. One brother and sister, whose names have been lost, wrote a diary in the margins of a French novel. In an undated entry, the boy writes: "My little sister complains of losing the will to live. How tragic. She is only twelve years old! Will there be an end to our suffering? When and how, great heavens? Humanity, where are you!" In another passage he writes that he wants to live so that he can ensure the Nazis are punished: "I go on dreaming, dreaming about survival and about getting free in order to be able to 'tell' the world, to yell and 'rebuke,' to tell and to protest." Neither the boy nor his sister survived.

Even in those hopeless ghettos, parents and teachers tried to educate children. Ben Gildadi was given lessons in the Piotrkow ghetto by Hela Rosenbaum, a teacher from Warsaw who shared his family's apartment. For a while Ben was the only pupil, but soon there were eight children, all sitting in the small attic room with its curved ceiling and narrow window. In the middle of the room was a table where the children worked, and above the bed hung a small blackboard. It wasn't just the lessons that Ben valued; it was the feeling Hela gave him that he was "equal to all the youngsters who were free."

The children were taught literature, history, Latin, mathematics, physics, and Hebrew. This was all strictly forbidden by the Nazis, and so the teacher told the children to come into class one by one, carrying their books under their clothes. Sometimes the SS appeared downstairs, and the children had to flee the attic schoolroom. In 1942, most of the pupils were sent to labor camps, Ben among them. He survived the war, but his teacher, Hela, was killed by the Nazis.

Lorraine Justman-Wisnicki, a teacher in the Gorzkowice ghetto, helped children write their own newspaper. Their greatest achievement as a group was the play they performed for the entire ghetto population. It was a huge success, both for the children who sang and danced and acted, and for their audience. For the brief time of the play, they had hope. But none of the young performers or any-one in the crowd was to survive the war.

Thousands of Jews from the ghettos were put to work in slave-labor camps. They produced everything from uniforms to hand grenades. They lived and worked in appalling conditions, in places without proper sanitation, with hardly any food and very little rest. Over half a mil-lion Jews, including many children, died while working as slave laborers.

Visiting the Franks' apartment in the spring of 1940, Miep was astonished to see how quickly Margot and Anne were growing up. Margot was now a young lady rather than a girl, and had lost the slight plumpness of her childhood to become tall and willowy. She had beautiful skin and dark, clever eyes behind her glasses. She concentrated on her schoolwork and was usually very serious. Anne admired her, despite the jealousy she sometimes felt of her elder sister, and copied her as much as possible. Anne had developed into a skilled mimic, and would imitate everyone she knew, from the teachers at school to her friends, perfectly capturing their mannerisms and voices. She loved to make people laugh and to have an attentive audience. Miep realized that Anne was going through a sudden spurt of growth; she was still very thin, but her arms and legs seemed much longer. Yet Anne remained the baby of the family and loved to get any extra attention.

The Franks went to a professional photographer every year to record their children growing up. Anne later stuck the photos of herself from 1940 into her diary. In them, she sits hunched up, her arms folded, with her hair pinned up at the sides. She is smiling in most, looking above or to the side. She captioned them: "Things are getting more serious, but there's still a smile left over from the funny bits"; "Oh, what a joke"; "Whatever next?"; "That's a funny story"; "Nice one, as well." On one photograph she lifts her head slightly and looks deep in thought. She wrote next to it in black pen: "This is a photograph of me as I wish I looked all the time. Then I might still have a chance of getting into Holywood [sic]. But at present, I'm afraid, I usually look quite different."

These were the last days of freedom, although Anne did not know it then. Hitler was planning to conquer more countries in his bid for world domination, and in the early hours of May 10, 1940, German forces invaded Holland.

FIVE:
"WHEN THE SUFFERINGS OF US JEWS REALLY BEGAN . . ."

Margot Frank's best friend Jetteke Frijda remembers, "The day after the invasion was a school day. We were called into the large assembly hall and were told that we were at war with Germany. We were sent home and didn't come back until after the surrender." Four days passed between the German invasion and the surrender of the Dutch forces. In that time, the Germans threatened to bomb the city of Rotterdam if the Dutch armed forces continued to fight. Two hours before the deadline, the Germans bombed Rotterdam anyway. The city was virtually wiped out, killing hundreds and making many thousands homeless. Holland surrendered on May 14, 1940. The Dutch royal family and the government fled to London.

In a massive convoy, the Germans entered sun-drenched Amsterdam, grinning and waving from their army cars and trucks. One hundred seventy thousand Jews lived in Holland, most of them in Amsterdam. Having read newspaper reports about the treatment of Jews in Poland, they were understandably frightened, and many tried to escape the country, while others committed suicide. Yet at the beginning of the occupation, life went on much as it always had, apart from the air raids. Eva Geiringer was a young girl who lived opposite the Franks on the Merwedeplein, and she recalls: "During the invasion there were aeroplanes coming over from both sides. We were terrified by all the bombing and shooting. It was the first war *we* encountered, and it was extremely frightening. But with the surrender, things almost became normal again. We went back to our schools and it wasn't too bad for us Jewish people or anybody else. Enough food and so on. It came gradually." Eva had arrived recently from Brussels with her parents and older brother.

In August, the Franks took their usual day trips to Zandvoort. Anne had fallen in love with a fourteen-year-old boy called Peter Schiff. She later wrote of him in her diary: "Peter crossed my path and in my childish way I really fell in love. He also liked me very much and we couldn't be parted for one whole summer. I can still see us walking hand in hand through the streets together. . . . I would often fetch him from school, or he would fetch me and I often went to his house. Peter was a very good-looking boy, tall, handsome and slim, with an earnest,

Margot (standing) and Anne at Zandvoort, 1940.

calm, intelligent face. . . . When he laughed, a naughty glint came into his eye." When one of Peter's friends teased him about Anne (she was eleven years old, three years younger than Peter), he began to ignore her. Anne was miserable at first, but her home and social life were too busy for her to stay depressed for long.

On December 1, 1940, Mr. Frank's businesses, Opekta and Pectacon, moved to 263 Prinsengracht, in the pretty Jordaan area of Amsterdam. The ground floor of the building was used as a warehouse, while the first floor became offices. A steep staircase led up to the second floor, where large mixing containers, sacks of jam-making ingredients, and spices were kept. The attics above were also used for storage. Like many canal-side houses, the building had an annex at the back. The second and third floors of the annex were not used, but Mr. Frank converted the open space on the first floor into two rooms for his private office and the staff kitchen.

The Nazis had begun closing down businesses run by Jews, so Mr. Frank did two things to keep his companies safe. He changed the name of Pectacon, with Jan Gies's help, to Gies & Co., and he pretended that he was no longer head of the company. He did a similar thing with Opekta, resigning from the company and asking Johannes Kleiman to replace him. In fact, Mr. Frank was in charge as he had always been, but the Nazis, not realizing this, allowed Pectacon and Opekta to function as usual.

———

Although the Nazis had been slow to pass anti-Jewish laws in Holland at first, at the start of 1941 things began to change. In February, Jews of all ages living in Holland had to register. This was done so that the Nazis could find out exactly how many Jews lived in the country, where they were, and who they were. Street violence against Jews rose sharply, and during one fight a well-known Dutch Nazi was injured and later died from his wounds. In revenge, a large group of Nazis marched into the old Jewish Quarter in Amsterdam and rounded up all the men and boys they could find, then beat them savagely before sending them away in trucks. No one knew where they had gone.

As a protest against the roundup, the Communist Party organized a strike in several major Dutch cities. For two days, streetcars remained in their depots, office workers stood outside in the watery sunshine, and all the harbors and steel plants closed down. Furious, the Germans threatened to punish everyone involved in the strike. Reluctantly, everyone returned to work.

The shadow cast by the Nazi occupation seemed to grow longer with each passing day. The anti-Jewish laws came in one after the other in 1941, preventing Jews from doing their jobs and enjoying a social life. The non-Jewish Dutch population in general did little to object. They were either too afraid or did not particularly care. As a result, Jews became more and more isolated.

June 12, 1941, was Anne's twelfth birthday. She wrote to Omi in Switzerland at the end of the month, explaining that she would have written sooner but her birthday celebrations had been postponed because Oma Hollander had been in the hospital. She told Omi about the presents she had received and added: "Soon we'll have the holidays. I'm going with Sanne Lederman to a children's camp, which makes it not so lonely. Yesterday (Sunday) I was out with Sanne, Hanneli and a boy. I can't complain of a lack of boyfriends. We don't have much chance to get tanned any more because we can't go to the swimming pool [this was one of the anti-Jewish laws]. It's a pity, but that's how it is."

Anne went to summer camp with Sanne, as she had told her grandmother. Her father, mother, and Margot joined her there in July. When they returned home, Miep and Jan announced that they were getting married. Everyone was invited, but Oma Hollander was seriously ill with cancer, and Margot also had an illness of some sort. Edith stayed at home to look after them, but Anne attended the wedding with her father. She had a new suit and a matching cloche hat with a ribbon for the occasion. Her hair had been cut in a bob, and she looked every inch the chic young girl her friends admired. The weather was fine, and a street photographer took snaps of the wedding party. The following day, Mr. Frank gave a reception for the couple at the Prinsengracht offices. Anne and Bep prepared the food and acted as waitresses. When Miep and Jan visited the Franks at their home soon afterward, Miep noticed that "in addition to Anne's many interests, like the cinema, famous film stars, and her best girlfriends, a new subject had got her attention—boys. . . . It was as though the terrible events in the outside world were speeding up this little girl's development, as though Anne was suddenly in a hurry to know and experience everything. On the outside, Anne looked like a delicate, vivacious girl, but on the inside, a part of her was suddenly much older."

A new law brought in that summer ordered the separation of Jewish children and non-Jewish children in school. Anne and Margot, together with all the Jewish children at their school, were called into a special assembly. They were told that they would have to transfer to the new Jewish school. Anne wept when she had to say good-bye to Mrs. Kuperus, the headmistress. Later, Otto Frank recalled how, under the new law, "it was very difficult for Anne and Margot to keep up their friendships with non-Jewish children, particularly now that it was forbidden for Christians to visit Jewish families and vice versa. . . . When I think back to the time when a lot of laws were introduced in Holland, which made our lives a lot harder, I have to say that my wife and I did everything we could to stop the children noticing the trouble we would go to, to make sure this was still a trouble-free time for them."

Anne and Margot were transferred to the Jewish Lyceum, a three-story building with a long concrete playground in front and one at the back. An archway at the front led through to the Amstel River. Laureen Klein, a friend of Margot's, remembers seeing Anne at the streetcar stop every morning now that they had changed schools: "We lived two stops beyond the Franks. Anne and her entourage would get on the streetcar and I would think, 'Isn't she lively?' She definitely was the center of the circle. Talk, talk, talk." Anne went into the first form of the Lyceum with Lies Goslar, and Margot went into the fourth with Jetteke Frijda.

Anne found a new best friend at the Lyceum, Jacqueline van Maarsen, who also lived in the River Quarter. The two girls became very close and found that they shared many of the same interests, and could spend hours sitting on the flat roof of Anne's apartment, chattering about all kinds of things. They even organized film shows together, sending out tickets to their school friends, who were then invited to Anne's home to watched a rented film on the Franks' old projector. Jacqueline remembers, "Anne made everything fun. I have never met anyone else since then who enjoyed life as my friend Anne did. Anne was the one with the movie star collection [postcards], and I helped her with it. When we stayed at each other's house, it was Anne who decided about that. We alternated—not every night of course, just sometimes—but Anne always invited herself. She was pretty, too. The photograph that everyone knows—where she sits at a desk with her arms folded—isn't her best picture. She had a brace on her teeth then and was trying to hide it. She looked much nicer than that."

Although Anne sometimes complained about her mother and sister, Jacqueline thought that they were "always very sweet to Anne and patient with her. . . . Margot was very nice to Anne always. She really was 'the big sister.' I suppose I looked up to her, like my own sister. Margot was very clever, but I don't think I really noticed that then. I never saw any rivalry between them. Margot was always very nice to Anne, and Anne wasn't always nice, but she was never unpleasant with Margot." Anne never complained about her father, but then the two of them were similar. Jacqueline remembers: "Otto was an extrovert, just like his daughter Anne. . . . She always had to have someone around to talk to or play with or else she became bored."

Just after Jacqueline and Anne first met, Mr. Frank took Anne out of school for a couple of days to go on a short trip to Arnhem. He sent a postcard to his mother from there on September 14, 1941: "Dearest mother, Anne and I have traveled here for a couple of days, the

Jacqueline van Maarsen

others stopped in Amsterdam. We're not staying long, I just wanted to have a bit more peace and quiet, but didn't want to go off completely on my own. Anne is always good, dear company and she was able to have a few days off school. Everything is well. All our love to everyone, yours Otto." The front of the card showed their hotel, the Groot Warnsborn, and across it Anne wrote happily: "We're staying here! In the middle of the forest! Isn't it wonderful?"

When Hitler's forces invaded Russia on June 22, 1941, right behind the troops were the *Einsatzgruppen*, specialist Nazi soldiers whose main task was to murder as many Jews as they could. They entered towns and villages, rounding up Jews, then took them out to forests or ravines to shoot them. Sometimes local people would help the Einsatzgruppen with these murders. The victims were buried in mass graves. At a place called Babi Yar, just outside the city of Kiev, over 30,000 Jewish men, women, and children were killed by the Einsatzgruppen in two days. Afterward, Jewish slave laborers were made to burn the bodies to hide all evidence of the crime. Another 8,000 Jews who had been in hiding and imprisoned in slave-labor camps were later killed at Babi Yar. The largest number of Jews killed by the Einsatzgruppen was at Drobitsky Yar, where over 40,000 people were killed.

By now, German forces also occupied Denmark, Norway, Holland, Belgium, Luxembourg, France, Romania, and Yugoslavia. The Einsatzgruppen in Russia had proved so successful in their task that Hitler felt certain his secret plans for Jews in the other countries under his control could now become reality. In the summer of 1941, Heinrich Himmler told his men: "The Führer has given the order for a final solution to the Jewish question and we, the SS, must carry out that order."

But it wasn't until early the following year that the plans were fully explained to the Nazi officials who would be in charge of carrying them out. Hitler's "Final Solution"— the extermination of every Jewish man, woman, and child in Europe—was presented to fifteen senior Nazi and German officials at a top secret meeting on January 20, 1942, at a villa on the shores of Lake Wannsee, close to Berlin. Among the men there that day were Adolf Eichmann (Head of the Gestapo's Jewish Affairs section) and Heinrich Müller (Head of the Gestapo). All were gathered there on the orders of Reinhard Heydrich, who described how the Final Solution would take place, and what he expected of the men sitting before him. He told them that in order to ensure the destruction of the Jews in Nazi-occupied territory, "Europe will be combed from east to west." Eventually, these plans would include Jews living beyond Nazi control; Adolf Eichmann handed around a list of countries (among them England and the Republic of Ireland) and the number of Jews living in each one. When the meeting was over, Eichmann, Heydrich, and Müller sat by the fireside, drinking cognac and smoking cigars.

What the fifteen officials were told that day in the villa at Lake Wannsee was this: Jews would be shipped from every country under Nazi control to special camps where they would be murdered. Throughout Germany and much of Poland, concentration camps for forced labor already existed. Under the Final Solution, these camps would take on a different role, new camps would be built, and almost every prisoner entering the camps would be killed. Experiments in murdering large numbers of people had already occurred before the meeting at Lake Wannsee. These took place in a camp called Auschwitz.

Auschwitz lay close to the small Polish manufacturing village of Oswiecim, where the Sola and Vistula rivers entwine in marshy, barren acres of land. Auschwitz was the name given to it by the Germans, who chose it for its easy rail access; Auschwitz was a main junction taking people to and from all the European capitals. But it was also an isolated spot. Thirty convicted German criminals were sent to Auschwitz on May 5, 1940, to serve as Kapos (head prisoners who acted as guards). Together with 300 local Jews, they began to prepare the site.

Rudolf Höess, a devout Roman Catholic, became Commandant of Auschwitz on May 1, 1940, and remained there until 1943. In the summer of 1941, Adolf Eichmann

Adolf Hitler and German chief of police, Heinrich
Himmler (left), watching Stormtroop maneuvers.

visited the camp to talk to Höess about killing techniques, including murder by gas. Heinrich Himmler also called on Höess to tell him about the Final Solution, adding that "Auschwitz would serve as the center of destruction." At the end of the meeting, Himmler confided, "Every Jew that we can lay our hands on is to be destroyed now."

On September 3, 1941, 850 prisoners, 600 of whom were Russian prisoners of war, were taken to a cellar in Auschwitz. They were gassed using Zyklon B, the trade name of a chemical used in pest control, tiny blue-green crystals that dissolved on contact with air, releasing a deadly gas. The crystals were dropped in through vents in the ceiling of the gas chamber. There was no possibility of survival.

After the meeting at the villa on Lake Wannsee in 1942, instructions for enlarging Auschwitz I Main Camp were given. The building of Birkenau, the camp's killing terminal, started in the fall. *Birkenau* is German for Birch Wood, which is where it was situated, across the railway line from Auschwitz I. There were many sub-camps within it: a women's camp, a men's camp, a gypsy camp, medical huts, etc. There were also gas chambers, undressing rooms, crematoriums, and pits where bodies could be burned. Electrified barbed wire surrounded the camp, with towers where armed guards constantly kept watch. Later it was enlarged again; Auschwitz III consisted of the surrounding sub-camps and factories dealing in everything from coal mining to agriculture. Within three years, Auschwitz covered twenty-five square miles of barracks, factories, and killing compounds.

Jews living in Polish ghettos were the first to be deported. They were rounded up and put on trains, traveling under the impression that they were being resettled for work in labor camps. In the Warsaw ghetto, where starvation was rife, Jewish families were lured to the death camp of Treblinka with the promise of something as simple as bread and jam. Most concentration camps were fitted with gas chambers. Told that they were being taken into showers or to be disinfected, groups of twenty or thirty were led into the chambers.

The diary of David Rubinowicz, a young boy deported from Poland, has survived. David began keeping his diary in 1940. In 1942 he wrote about the order to "evacuate," which meant all Jews in his town were to be deported. Earlier that day he stood outside watching the wind tear through the fields and he saw the village watchman putting up a notice. David went to see what it said, and the watchman told him about the forthcoming evacuation. When he got home, David told his family about the notice. Everyone had the same question: Where would they end up?

David's diary ends abruptly, as he is describing the murder of two Jewish women: "They went out into the woods and shot them there. The Jewish police immediately went to bury them in the cemetery. When the cart returned it was full of blood. Who . . ." David was deported to Treblinka. He died in the gas chambers there, shortly before his fifteenth birthday.

In general, there were few children in the concentration camps. There were two main reasons: Children could not work as hard as adults, and they also represented the future of the Jewish people. In most camps, selections were made immediately after the trains pulled into the compounds (usually at night, to confuse the exhausted passengers). The old, the sick, pregnant women, and children under the age of fifteen were almost always sent straight to the gas chambers. Teenagers who managed to, convince SS officers that they had a trade (for example, that they were trained electricians), were allowed into the camps along with those who appeared fit enough to work. But even among the workforce in the camps there were regular selections for the gas chambers. In Auschwitz, where approximately one million Jews died, Dr. Josef Mengele, the SS officer in charge of making the selections on the railway ramp, chose a number of children for his so-called medical experiments. When he no longer needed them, the children were sent to the gas chambers.

In January of 1942, Oma Hollander died. Anne and Margot were devastated by their grandmother's death, and Anne later wrote in her diary: "No one will ever know how much she is in my thoughts, and how much I love her still." She missed her grandmother's support; Oma Hollander had always been able to calm the often difficult relationship between Anne and Mrs. Frank.

In April of 1942, the Franks celebrated Passover with the van Pels family. Otto Frank's thoughts were on the future. In a letter written many years later, he explained, "I soon realized that the time would come when we would have to go into hiding to escape the deportations. After having discussed the matter thoroughly with Mr. van Pels, we came to the conclusion that the best solution would be to hide in the annex of our office building. This would only be possible if Mr. Kleiman and Mr. Kugler would be willing to take full responsibility for everything connected with our hiding, and if the two secretaries of the firm [Miep and Bep] would cooperate. All four immediately agreed, although they were fully aware of the dangerous task they would take upon themselves in doing so. By Nazi law, everyone helping Jews was severely punished and risked being put into prison, to be deported or even shot. During the following months we prepared the hiding place."

The annex was thoroughly cleaned out and cleared of debris. Food, bedclothes, soap, towels, and kitchen utensils were easy to move. Furniture and other large items were picked up in a van owned by Mr. Kleiman's brother and taken to the hiding place after office hours. All work done in the annex took place gradually, on weekends and in the evenings. Paper was pasted over the windows in the front house facing the annex, shielding the rooms from the warehousemen and visitors to the office. The families would move in sometime in July of 1942.

Anne and Margot were not told immediately about the hiding plan; their father wanted them to enjoy what was left of their freedom. Children in general did not worry as their parents did. In her diary, Anne writes, "Jacque used to say to me, 'You're scared to do anything because it may be forbidden.'" But today Jacqueline remembers, "We talked about the laws as they came in, but not very much. The worst thing was not knowing what was going to happen next. All the time, there were new regulations, but you just got used to them."

During Easter in 1942, Anne discovered her bicycle had been stolen. Since Jews were now banned from using public transport, her only option was to walk everywhere. She now had half an hour's walk to school each day. The evenings were no longer restful either because British airplanes on their way to bomb Germany flew over Amsterdam every night. When the air-raid alarm sounded, everyone living on the Merwedeplein gathered together at the arched entrances to the apartments. Searchlights crossed the sky and the anti-aircraft guns boomed and flashed. Everyone was frightened. There was a man called Dr.

Beffie who lived nearby and would join them during an air raid, always with a piece of bread in his hand. He ate very slowly, and Anne always stared at him. Then one night, as the all-clear sounded, Anne turned to her young neighbor Toosje and said, "Good heavens, if I chewed so slowly I think I'd be hungry all my life!"

In her book of short stories written in the confines of the annex, Anne described this time in the section "Do You Remember? Reminiscences of My Schooldays." She mused, "That one year in the Lyceum was sheer bliss for me; the teachers, all they taught me, the jokes, the prestige, the romances, and the adoring boys." Otto noticed his daughter was becoming even more popular as she grew up: "She was always on the go, and always brought a whole community of children with her wherever she was. People loved her because she had ideas, what to play, where to play, some new things to do. . . . Anne had one quality that was a bit annoying. She was constantly asking questions, not only when we were alone, but also in the presence of others. When we had visitors, it was very difficult to get rid of her, because everyone and everything was of interest to her."

Anne, Lies, Jacqueline, Sanne, and Ilse Wagner (Lies's best friend from the Lyceum) formed a table-tennis club that summer called "The Little Bear Minus Two." Jacqueline recalls, "We formed the ping pong club because there was so little we were allowed to do, and also, children were not spoiled with choices like there are now." The odd name came about by mistake. They wanted to name the club after a constellation of stars, and thought that the Little Bear had five stars (like their group), but later discovered it in fact had seven, hence the "minus two." Mini-tournaments were held in the dining room of Ilse's home with her table-tennis set. Afterward, being "very partial to an ice cream," they would visit the Oasis ice cream parlor or the Delphi tearoom, both in the River Quarter. Jacqueline explains: "We never sat inside Oasis. The Jewish boys and girls from the neighborhood congregated there, but it was a social encounter played out on the pavement. One bought an ice cream and went outside to eat it. . . . We always ran into people we knew there. Anne loved walking behind boys and fantasizing that they were all her admirers."

In May of 1942, Anne wrote to congratulate Buddy on his seventeenth birthday. She told him, "I've been busy every day. This evening I won't get home until ten, but I'm usually escorted home by a young man. How's it going with your girlfriend, the one you sent a picture of? Please write more about her, things like that always interest me. Margot also has a boyfriend, but he's even younger than mine." Margot sent her own birthday greetings to their cousin, writing, "I said to Mummy yesterday how well I remember seeing you on Omi's birthday when we were ten years old. Hopefully we'll see each other before you're eighteen. . . . I don't think it's so nice to have your birthday on a weekday because you have to go to school all day, and now, next year, we will both have finished school. But who knows what will happen then."

SIX

"IT'S AN ODD IDEA FOR SOMEONE LIKE ME TO KEEP A DIARY . . ."

On April 29, 1942, Jews living in Holland, France, and Belgium were subjected to a new law that made them more visible than ever: the forced wearing of the Jewish Star of David. The German announcement read: "All Jews appearing in public must wear a Jewish star. The Jewish star shall be a black, six-pointed star on yellow material, the size of a palm, and bearing the inscription 'Jew.' The star shall be clearly visible and affixed to the outer clothing over the left breast; Jews are debarred from wearing orders, decorations and other insignia." Jews in Germany and Czechoslovakia had been wearing the star since September of 1941. Stars could only be bought from distribution centers and cost four cents and a stamp from the cloth-ration card, which limited the amount of cloth each person could buy. Refusal to wear the star resulted in a fine or imprisonment—and even Jews in jail had to wear them. Only children under the age of six or twelve (depending where they lived) were exempt.

Livia, a young Jewish girl living in Hungary was outraged at the idea of having to wear the star. She wrote in her diary: "I am not going to wear the yellow star! I am not going to appear in public with the Jew badge. I can't be seen wearing that horrible, horrible thing. I will die if any of my schoolmates see me. . . . I sat indoors for over a week. Mother pleaded, her voice gentle and sad, 'Elli, let us thank God for being alive. Let us thank God for being together, in our own house. What is a yellow star on a jacket? It does not kill or condemn. It does not harm. It only means you are a Jew. That is nothing to be ashamed of. We are not marked for being criminals. Only for being Jews. Aren't you proud of being a Jew?' I did not know if I was proud to be a Jew. I had never thought about it. But I knew I did not want to be marked as a Jew or anything else."

In Holland, a slogan was coined: "Wear It with Pride, the Yellow Star!" Some Jews *were* proud of their star, but others were ashamed. When they were first issued, some non-Jews, outraged at this latest anti-Jewish law, wore them in protest. The Gestapo threatened them with deportation. The Nazis did not make idle threats, as an event in June of 1942 made clear.

On May 27, SS chief Reinhard Heydrich was mortally wounded in an assassination attempt in the Czechoslovakian city of Prague. He died from his wounds on June 4. In revenge, the Nazis made an example of one community. On the evening of June 9, 1942, SS troops stormed into the village of Lidice, thirteen miles from Prague. The men of Lidice were marched to a barn where they were shot. Some were no more than fifteen years old. Seven women who had refused to leave their husbands were also killed. The rest of Lidice's population— 196 women and 105 children—were driven in trucks to the nearby town of Kladno. The SS burned Lidice to the ground. (In 1946, work began on rebuilding the village, with money donated from all over the world. Survivors of that night still live in Lidice, where there is now a museum telling the story of June 9, 1942.) From Kladno, the women were sent to the Ravensbruck concentration camp, and most of the children were sent to Chelmno to be gassed. Those children whose blood was "pure" enough were sent to Germany to be trained as good Nazi children. Only seventeen of Lidice's 105 children were traced after the war. Most of the women survived, but none of them ever saw their children again.

Elsewhere, a rash of new anti-Jewish laws made life almost unbearable for those caught in the Nazi web. Eva Geiringer, whose family were neighbors of the Franks, recalls: "People always say nowadays, why did you do this and why did you do that, but we were so scared. We thought, if we do the things that are demanded of us, we'll be all right. You're told to have a 'J' on your passport, you go and do it. Especially in a smaller community like Amsterdam where everybody knows who is Jewish and who comes from where. We thought, if we wear the star, if we obey the curfew, if we *do* everything, nothing will happen to us."

Fifteen-year-old Esther van Vriesland, also living in Holland, began keeping a diary in 1942. On June 14, she wrote: "We were still in bed yesterday, when mother came in with the newspaper. There were all sorts of new regulations: no more canoeing, rowing, swimming, and fishing. In one word: awful. How to spend the holiday now? Bicycles have to be handed in. This I don't mind too much. I don't feel like a holiday at all anymore. I looked forward to the holidays so much! Horrid, that's what it is." At the end of the month, Esther wrote in her diary again: "I am so terribly miserable. New regulation: we can't go out after eight o'clock at night till six o'clock in the morning. Shopping between three and five in the afternoon. Holding of certain professions forbidden, no more public transport, so from now on we have to walk. . . . And for persons with a travel permit: wait until everyone else is on the train and only sit down when all non-Jews have found a seat. Otherwise, stand up. O God, how humiliating. When I heard about it for the first time I could have cried. Even now, but then I felt so rebellious. Will it never end?" Esther was deported three months later. She died in the gas chambers at Auschwitz. The last line of her diary read: "Please, let me write about peace in the next notebook."

Friday, June 12, 1942, was Anne's thirteenth birthday. Her father took her to Blankevoorts, a large bookstore around the corner from her house, to choose a present. Anne picked out a diary—actually a red-and-white-checked autograph album—from the books and stationery on sale. Lies arrived early that morning to pick up Anne for school, and admired the diary briefly before Anne put it away in her bedroom. In the sitting room, all of Anne's other presents were on display, and there were flowers everywhere. In the kitchen, her mother was baking a strawberry pie, while her father sat comfortably in his chair and shared a joke with Lies as usual. When it was time to leave, Mrs. Frank gave Anne a basket of cookies to hand out at school, and Anne added some cookies she had made. In the afternoon, Lies, Jacqueline, Sanne, and Ilse gave Anne their joint gift, a book called *Tales and Legends of the Netherlands*.

At some point on her birthday, Anne wrote in the diary for the first time. She pasted in a school photograph of herself from the winter of 1941 with the caption, "Gorgeous photograph, isn't it!!!!" At the front of the book she wrote, "I hope I shall be able to confide in you completely, as I never have in anyone before, and I hope that you will

Anne writing at her desk, 1941.

be a great support and comfort to me." All Anne's friends were aware that she had been given a diary. Lies comments, "I remember that Anne was always writing in her diary, shielding it with her hand, even at school during the break. Everybody could see that she was writing. But no one was allowed to see what she had written." Jacqueline agrees: "We were very curious about it . . . we wanted to see what she had written about us." She also remembers Anne had an unusual way of writing: "Anne always wrote with her pen between her index finger and her middle finger because she had sprained her finger at some point. I had always admired her handwriting and tried to imitate it by holding my pen the same way."

Anne's party was held on the Sunday after her birthday, and Jacqueline's strongest memory of the day is of Anne's happiness at being surrounded by her friends: "With sparkling eyes she had watched her friends enter and opened her presents expectantly. She had enjoyed being the center of attention." Lies recalls the gaggle of children in the apartment, Anne's parents handing out slices of strawberry pie on china plates, glasses of cool milk for everyone, Margot and Jetteke Frijda joining in with them all, the blinds being pulled down as Mr. Frank set up the projector, and then *Rin-Tin-Tin and the Lighthouse Keeper* whirring into life on the blank wall. Lies also remembers having to leave the party early to help her mother with her baby sister Gabi, and her feelings of jealousy when she saw Anne and Jacqueline whispering together. She thought of that moment in the months that followed and always told herself, "If I'd known what was going to happen, I wouldn't have minded."

By the end of June, Anne had a new boyfriend, Hello (Edmond) Silberberg. Hello was also from Germany and had arrived in the River Quarter in 1938. He lived with his grandparents and was a handsome sixteen-year-old when his cousin introduced him to Anne. He remembers, "She was very attractive and she liked to laugh and to make people laugh. She was very entertaining and extremely lively. She did little imitations of people that were very clever. In my memory I always see her sitting in a big chair, with her hands under her chin and looking directly at whomever she was with. . . . I think I was probably in love with her. She seemed to think so too." Anne's parents liked Hello, but his grandparents disapproved of her; they thought she was too young for him and didn't like the fact that Hello had left his previous girlfriend for her. Anne worried about this and questioned him about their future together. He told her, "Love finds a way!"

At the end of the school year, the children received their test scores. Margot's were excellent as usual, and Anne's were better than she had expected, although she and Lies would have to retake the math test in September. Around this time, Mr. Frank told Anne about the hiding plan. Margot already knew, and Anne confided in her diary her impassioned hope that "the fulfilment of these somber words remain far distant yet."

Although she had no way of knowing it then, Anne paid her last visit to Jacqueline and her family during the first week of July, when she arrived at the van Maarsens' flat on Hunzestraat to show off a new dress. Mrs. van Maarsen told her that it looked very sweet on her. Anne smiled and replied, "Why of course it does. It's brand new."

The morning of Sunday, July 5, 1942, was sunny and hot. Anne's father walked to the Jewish hospital in town to visit some of the elderly patients there, leaving Anne and Margot at home with their mother. Hello called around to make arrangements with Anne for an outing later that afternoon. When he had gone, Anne stretched out on the terrace to read. At three o'clock the doorbell rang and there was a call from the street, "Miss Margot Frank?" Mrs. Frank went down to answer it. A policeman handed her a registered envelope.

Inside was a card ordering Margot to report to the SS the next morning.

At the end of June of 1942, Adolf Eichmann had informed all departments involved in the Final Solution that in July, mass deportations to the extermination camps in the east would begin.

The Nazi government decided to deport 4,000 Jews

in Holland to "German work camps." The first call-up notices were sent out to German Jews on Sunday, July 5, 1942. The notices didn't explain where they were going or what they could expect; all that was included was a list of clothing to be taken in a backpack. The Jewish Council in Amsterdam urged people to obey the call-ups, fearing what might happen if too many resisted, and advised them to comply "in your own interests . . . [W]hat you will be asked to do is ordinary relief work. . . ." Most of those receiving the call-up on July 5 were German Jews, like Margot, aged fifteen and sixteen.

If the people receiving the call-up notices did not report as ordered, then the Nazis would simply pick Jews to be taken away at random. Often, Nazis barricaded neighborhoods while all houses were searched for Jews. Dotje Cohen, who was very young and living with her foster parents, remembers the night SS men turned up in her street: "They closed off the street and turned huge spot-lights toward the apartment houses. Papa Is and Annie [foster parents] lifted me onto a narrow folding bed and strapped me securely to the mattress. Then they closed me into the closet and told me not to make a sound. I could hear the Gestapo's loud stomping boots on the stairs and the banging on the door. They came in and searched everywhere. They even opened the closet where I was and for a moment I froze. Then they closed the door and left without saying a word. I was safe once again." The

Nazis later returned looking for Dotje, and broke into the house, shouting her name. They pushed aside her foster father, who tried to fight them, until they reached Dotje: "One of the soldiers . . . started pushing me down the stairs. The stairs were dark and I couldn't see; I kept stumbling. . . . I didn't feel the bitter cold because I was afraid. I was more afraid the night they took me away from my foster family than I have ever been in my whole life." Dotje survived, but she never forgot the fear she felt that night.

In Holland, Jews were sent either straight to the railway station for deportation or to the Hollandsche Schouwburg, an old theater close to the city zoo. Below its ornate ceilings, Jewish men, women, and children lay slumped on the floor for days, some dying of thirst and hunger. There was no fresh air and only dull, artificial light. A Dutch historian explains: "There were screaming children everywhere, in the corridors, in the halls, in the foyers, the balconies, the pit, the staircases, the stalls. Then there were those who could not lie still and kept walking about the building."

Ironically, the terrible conditions in the theater led to over one thousand Jewish children being saved. The theater was so overcrowded that the Nazis decided to send children to stay in the Jewish nursery directly across the street. The director there, Henriette Rodriquez-Pimentel, and the young Jewish women who worked for her, rescued as many children as they could. Although newcomers to the nursery had to be registered by the Jewish Council, all the files on the children were destroyed by nursery assistant Walter Süsskind and Felix Halverstad, who worked at the Council. The children could not be traced. They were then smuggled out of the nursery in several ways. The nursery assistants would take toddlers and older children out on walks and then meet a member of a resistance group who would bring them to safety. (Resistance groups secretly worked together against the Nazis, forging documents, finding hiding places, and smuggling reports on what was happening in the country to those in the free world.) Babies were secretly carried out in backpacks, potato sacks, and laundry baskets. Next door to the nursery was a teacher-training college whose director, Professor van Hulst, also wanted to help. Children were dropped carefully over the wall of the nursery into the garden of the college, where someone would be waiting to take them to a safe address. One of the children saved by the nursery staff, Ed van Thijn, later became the mayor of Amsterdam.

Jewish children were not the only ones to be deported, although they formed the largest group of children sent to the concentration camps. The second largest group of children in the camps belonged to Roma and Sinti families. In 1940, all Roma and Sinti families still living in Germany had been sent east to Poland to live in ghettos there. When mass deportations of Jews from the ghettos to the death camps began, Roma and Sinti were also included. After the war, it was estimated that approximately half a million Roma and Sinti had been killed in the camps in total—almost the entire Roma and Sinti population of Eastern Europe.

Throughout 1942 and 1943, the deportation trains rolled out from Europe's major cities. There was only one way to avoid the dreaded transport, for all other avenues of escape had long been closed: to go into hiding.

As soon as Margot received the call-up, Mrs. Frank left home to tell the van Pelses that the hiding plan would have to be brought forward. At first, Margot told Anne that the SS had sent a call-up for their father, but then she told her the truth. Anne began to cry. Hello returned at the same time as Mrs. Frank and Hermann van Pels. He was told that Anne couldn't see him just then, and Jacqueline was told something similar when she telephoned later. Anne and Margot were sent to their room to begin packing. Anne put her diary and old letters into a satchel. They were more important to her than clothes. She still did not know where their hiding place would be.

Anne's father returned from visiting friends at five o'clock. When he was given the news, he called Mr. Kleiman, who came over immediately. Miep and Jan Gies came to take the Franks' belongings—mostly clothes and toiletries—to their own home for safekeeping until they were in the hiding place. An atmosphere of panic and fear made everyone much quieter than usual. The Franks' lodger, Mr. Goldschmidt, called on them that evening. He knew nothing of the hiding plan. He stayed until ten o'clock, and an hour later, Miep and Jan returned to take away more items and clothing. When they had gone, Mr. Frank wrote to his family in Switzerland, hinting that they were going into hiding:

"We are all well and together, that's the main thing. Everything is difficult these days, but you just have to take some things with a pinch of salt. I hope we'll find peace this year already so that we can see one another again. It's a pity we can no longer correspond with you, but that's how it is. You must understand." Anne added her last greetings: "I cannot write a letter about the holidays now. Regards and kisses from Anne."

It was eleven thirty when they went to bed. Anne was exhausted and fell asleep instantly.

It was raining the next morning as the family ate breakfast in the semi-darkness of five thirty A.M. They each wore as much clothing as possible to lessen the amount they had to carry. Margot filled her satchel with schoolbooks and pulled out her bike to wait for Miep, who arrived at six o'clock on her bicycle. They rode off across Merwedeplein silently. Mr. and Mrs. Frank left a letter for the lodger, asking him to take Anne's cat, Moortje, to their neighbors. They left the beds unmade and scat-

tered the breakfast things on the table as if they had had
to leave suddenly. At seven thirty A.M. they set off on foot
in the warm rain. The streets were dark, and cars sped
by, their headlights blurred by the downpour. As they
walked, Anne's father told her about the hiding place.

Margot and Miep were the first to arrive at the annex.
Margot was close to fainting. Miep remembers: "We were
soaked through to the skin. I could see that Margot was
on the verge of crumbling. . . . I gripped her arm to give
her courage. Still we said nothing. She disappeared behind
the door and I took my place in the front office. My heart,
too, was thumping." When Anne and their parents reached
the building later that morning, drenched by the rain and
tired by the long walk, they went straight upstairs to the
annex. Margot was waiting for them.

The annex was a mess, with boxes and sacks piled up
everywhere. In Mr. and Mrs. Frank's room there were two
divans, three tables, bookshelves, a built-in cupboard, and
150 cans of food. A window overlooked the courtyard
below and the houses opposite. A door to the right led to
Anne and Margot's narrow room. It had a window, two
divan beds, and three built-in cupboards. Next door was
a bathroom with a toilet. A doorway on the right led back
into the passageway and to the entrance door. On the
floor above was a large room with double windows looking
out onto the courtyard again. This was set aside for Mr.
and Mrs. van Pels. It was almost bare, apart from a sink,

cupboards, a gas stove, two beds, and a table. Another door led into the tiny damp room where Peter van Pels would sleep. There was a small shuttered window facing the front house, and the stairs to the attic in the middle of the room, along with a bed and a cupboard. From the arched side window in the attic, the tower of the Westerkerk (West Church) could be seen.

Visiting the annex later that day, Miep found Mrs. Frank and Margot lying on their beds in despair, but Anne and her father were busy trying to get things organized as quickly and quietly as possible. Miep could not imagine how they must have felt, but she was upset to see her friends forced to leave behind their home, their possessions, and their other friends. By then, the Franks' neighbors on Merwedeplein knew that they had gone. Jacqueline's mother remembered: "When we heard that the Franks were gone—to Switzerland, so we were told, a German army officer whom Mr. Frank had known in the first war was supposed to have taken them there—we were all glad, everyone I knew."

No one was surprised, because other families who had received the call-up notice had also disappeared. But Anne's friends were very upset when they heard; Lies and Jacqueline went straight to Anne's apartment and spoke to the Franks' lodger, Goldschmidt, who had spread the rumor of the family fleeing to Switzerland after finding a letter deliberately left by Mr. Frank hinting that this was what had happened. Jacqueline asked Goldschmidt whether they could have a last look around Anne's bedroom. He shrugged and let them in. Jacqueline and Lies walked around the room in a daze, not speaking. Jacqueline remembers seeing "Anne's unmade bed and on the floor in front of it, her new shoes, as if they had just been kicked off. . . . I saw *Variety*, the game she had just got for her birthday and which we had played like crazy the past few weeks, just lying there. . . ." They found Anne's swimming medals and took them; a few small reminders of the friend who had vanished.

SEVEN:

"WE HAVE TO WHISPER AND TREAD LIGHTLY . . ."

Approximately 100,000 children were hidden during the war. Every situation was different: Some children hid alone, some with their families, and some with strangers. They hid in the countryside and in cities. Some were hidden by a single person, some by a network of people. Occasionally children decided to go into hiding or on the run after their parents had been taken away in the roundups. But generally the arrangements to go into hiding were made by parents or guardians. It was unusual for an entire family to go into hiding together as the Frank family did; it seemed safer to separate, and it was easier to hide a single person than a group. A young child hiding alone could be passed off as a visiting relative or war orphan. For the children, this usually meant no contact at all with their real families; they were given new names and sometimes a new religion, and they were completely dependent upon the person caring for them.

Hiding places varied enormously, from city apartments above busy workplaces (as was the case with Anne and her family) to barns in the remote countryside. Hania Goldman (now Ann Shore) hid with her mother and sister in a Polish hayloft after her father was shot by German soldiers. Hania recalls: "Grudgingly, the farmer, a woman, let us stay, but she totally ignored us. We stayed for two and a half years. In all that time, she never gave us even a glass of water. . . . I could go out but only when there was no moon. If anyone saw me in the moonlight, I would have been killed. We had to whisper—for two and a half years we never once spoke above a whisper. . . . Each day, each night, brought fresh terror. It was a terrible existence in so many ways but as frightened as I was, I never even thought of giving up."

The sewers of Warsaw provided five-year-old Krystyna Chiger and her family with a hiding place. They managed to live in the wet and the dark with several other Jews and with large, reddish-colored rats and yellow worms crawling over the stones beneath their feet. Non-Jewish sewer workers gave them food and water. The people in hiding tried to avoid the rats, which spread disease and ate their bread. But Krystyna's little brother, Pawelek, loved the rats. To him, they were pets and he shared his food with them. One of the women hiding in the sewer cooked soup and

A child in the Warsaw ghetto, circa 1942.

coffee and offered some to Krystyna and her family. During the day, as water seeped down the walls, Krystyna listened to the cars driving on the street above them. She could hear people talking and children laughing and playing. She longed to join them. Miraculously, Krystyna and her family survived, though her brother was reluctant to go up into the daylight; he preferred the darkness of the sewer, which was the only home he remembered.

Wherever the hiding place itself was, the shock of being forced to actually go into hiding was enormous. It meant leaving behind all belongings and a way of life, loved ones, friends, community. Eva Geiringer, who hid with her mother while her father and brother found a separate hiding place, explains: "You couldn't imagine what it was like to go into hiding. Not to go out and see people—that's something that, as a child, you can't grasp. But when we actually went into hiding, that's when it started to sink in. I was very lively, I was thirteen, and had so much energy, but I just couldn't do anything. I was very afraid and very upset. I used to have wrestling matches with my mother to get rid of my energy. It was very, very hard."

Nothing and nowhere was safe; the smallest mistake might lead to discovery. In some houses, a second hiding place had been built in case of a Nazi raid. Children had to hide behind false walls in wardrobes, under floorboards, in mouse-infested attics. The most normal and basic activities became a problem in hiding; in her diary, Anne Frank writes of being able to flush the toilet only in certain hours, when they could be sure there was no one else in the building. If people visited the host family who didn't know there was someone hidden in the house, then the children had to be doubly careful. They were frightened, confused, and often terribly lonely.

Many children found refuge with religious institutions. They had no contact with their families and had to pretend to belong to the community where they were housed. Being forced to reject their own religion was something many older children found disturbing. Gisele Naichouler Feldman, then eleven years old, found shelter with the Catholic children's sanatorium in Chavaniac, France. She recalls: "A very difficult thing for me was having to attend a Catholic church every Sunday. I pretended to be a Catholic also, and even sang in the choir. I excused my ignorance of prayers and so did my brother by the explanations that our parents were not religious. I memorized all the necessary prayers but could not take the wafer. Still, every Sunday I felt like a fraud and had guilt feelings pretending to be someone I was not."

Some children felt guilty but understood that their safety depended upon their ability to blend in with the other children. Andy Sterling, a young Hungarian boy, was sent by his parents to hide in a Catholic orphanage. He arrived at the same time as another boy called Paul: "The priest and his assistant took Paul and me into an office and told us never to talk about being Jewish, not even to each other. . . . After the priest coached us on some of the morning prayers, he showed us to the dormitory. I lay in bed terrified. Everything was strange. I wanted my parents. . . . That morning I went to services and carefully watched what the others did. When they stood up, I stood up. When they knelt, I knelt. But when they crossed themselves, I felt uncomfortable. I had been brought up in a Jewish home and gone to Hebrew school and I felt awkward. In the end I crossed myself like the rest of the boys, and from then on I did what I was told. I was too afraid to do anything else." When the area was bombed, the pupils moved into the bunker for safety. They survived until liberation, and Andy was one of the few Jewish youngsters in hiding to be reunited with his family. Later he discovered there had been six other Jewish boys hiding in the orphanage besides himself and Paul.

Apart from the emotional difficulties of going into hiding, one of the most common practical problems was food. Resistance organizations forged ration books for people in hiding, who could not legally obtain them. As the war went on, certain foods became scarce, and during the Hunger Winter of 1944–1945 in Holland (when the Nazis cut off all electricity, and supplies and food could no longer be brought into the cities) some Jews in hiding died of starvation or illness. It was impossible to carry out the body normally; in several cases when a fugitive had died, the body was put inside a mattress to be taken out without arousing suspicion. Sometimes, in Amsterdam, bodies of Jews who had been in hiding and died were seen floating in the canals.

Discovery was the greatest fear, but being in hiding was also incredibly dull for normally active children. They passed the time painting, drawing, reading, writing, or studying. Gerry Mok was six years old when he was taken out of Amsterdam to hide in the Dutch town of Hoorn in February of 1942. Like other hidden children, he moved many times to avoid capture, and in some places, his host family started to teach him how to read and write. Gerry responded eagerly, anxious to continue with his lessons. Soon he was reading anything he could lay his hands on; it was a way of escaping reality, and he lived "partly in a dream world" through books.

Eva Geiringer was given lessons by her own mother while they were in hiding. She remembers: "From the time Mutti and I went into hiding, I entered a seemingly protected world. My days were spent entirely in the company of my mother and I remember them as full of warmth and love. During the next two years, hidden in our attic, she taught me German, French, geography and history. . . ."

Bertje van Rhijn, hiding in the Dutch town of Kampen with her family, was glad that the old lady who had agreed to shelter them had kept all her children's books, as well as their toys and games. Bertje discovered schoolbooks, atlases, novels, and biographies, and she read them all. The old lady was also a member of her local library, and borrowed books for her hidden guests. Bertje also kept a diary. Writing in a journal was also a way of preventing boredom. The van Rhijn family survived the war.

Moshe Flinker, another hidden child, used his journal to work out his opinions, his ambitions for the future, and the thoughts and feelings he preferred not to share with his family. Moshe was born in The Hague on October 9, 1926. His father was Polish but had emigrated to Holland, where he became a successful businessman. When the Flinkers received their call-up notice in July of 1942, they went into hiding in Brussels, across the border in occupied Belgium. There was no record of the family living there; they were able to hide "openly," using false identity papers.

In November of 1942, Moshe began to keep a diary. His religion was important to him, and he tried to understand the events unfolding around him in relation to God. On November 26, he worried about other Jews who had lost their faith: "They will think that there is no God at all in the universe, because had there been a God, He would not have allowed such things to happen to His people." Moshe, on the other hand, found that his belief in God gave him strength: "Had I not religion, I would never find any answer at all to all the problems that confront me." In July of 1943, he wrote: "I shall never stop hoping, because the moment I stop hoping I shall cease to exist. All

I have is hope; my entire being depends upon it."

Moshe's diary ended in September of 1943. A few months later, the Nazis raided the apartment where the Flinkers lived; they had been betrayed by a well-known Belgian collaborator. Moshe and his family were taken to Malines, the Belgian transit camp, and from there to Auschwitz, where he and his parents were gassed upon arrival. His brothers and sisters survived the war, and when they returned to their old apartment in Brussels, they found Moshe's diary and had it published.

Not all children in hiding had paper on which to write, or books to read. Some didn't have the energy or will to occupy themselves in this way; or they were made to work by their host families in the house, or if they lived in the countryside, on a farm. The difference in backgrounds between the hidden child and the host family also frequently created problems. Children whose parents were avid readers might be placed with a family who saw studying as wasteful when there was "real" work to be done, or the host family might be deeply religious and try to influence the hidden child into converting from Judaism. Although many hosts were kind and loving to the children they took in, some were not, acting out of greed and hoping to extract a lot of money from the parents of the child they were hiding. Generally, the younger the child, the more chance there was that the child and the host would bond. Older children could not forget their real parents and the lives they had led before the Nazis took away their freedom.

After the war, Jewish children who had been in hiding did not always want to go back to their real parents, even if they had survived. These children had grown attached to their foster families, and some were too young to remember their real parents. They suffered again when they had to leave their foster families and return to their real families. Their foster families often did not want them to go back either, which resulted in a battle for the child. Parents returning from the concentration camps sometimes found it difficult to get used to being with their children again after everything they had gone through. Some parents were unable to trace their children who had been placed with strangers, or who had moved from hiding place to hiding place. In those cases, children sometimes stayed with those who hid them; many did not even know that they were Jewish and that they had parents who had been killed in the concentration camps.

In all, eight people hid in the secret annex at 263 Prinsengracht: Anne and her family, the van Pelses, and from November of 1942, the dentist from Berlin, Fritz Pfeffer. They had to be extremely careful that no one else, apart from their helpers, knew that they were there. The door to the secret annex was concealed by a special bookcase that could be moved by those who knew where to look for its hidden hinges. Windows were covered by strips of thick material and blackout boards, used by everyone during wartime to confuse enemy bombers. There were certain rules that had to be strictly observed: The eight in hiding had to be as quiet as possible during office hours, the curtains were to be kept closed, the toilet was out of bounds when anyone else was in the building, and so on. Their fears of discovery were made worse by a number of burglaries that occurred at the offices during the period in hiding, and by the arrival of a new staff member in the warehouse, who became very curious about what was going on in the building.

Apart from their fears of being discovered, their biggest worry in hiding was food. Every morning, Miep and Bep gave the families their rations, which they collected on their behalf. Bread was bought from a friend of Mr. Kleiman, and a friend of Mr. van Pels provided them with meat. Miep visited a grocery store nearby for vegetables and became friendly with the owner, who was in the Dutch resistance. He soon guessed the reason for Miep's frequent visits to his shop, but he never gave away her secret. Bep was responsible for the milk ration and smuggled several bottles a day from the office supply to the annex. She also provided fruit for her friends in hiding when the prices were low. The attic quickly became a food store: Potatoes, peas, and other vegetables were kept there, along with lots of canned foods. In her diary, Anne sometimes grumbles about the lengthy food "cycles" they had to endure—weeks when only one or two types of food were available to them. As the war dragged on, Miep often spent hours waiting in line for groceries, only to be told at the counter that there was nothing left. Several major arguments broke out in the annex over the poor food and the way it was divided.

There were other practical difficulties. Soap, for example, was hard to find in the shops, and Miep or Bep had to give them what they could spare from their own rations once the original supply had dwindled. Washing was not a problem, since there was a sink in the annex, but taking a bath proved a little more difficult. Privacy was the main concern; each person chose his or her own place, using a portable tin washtub. Anne and Margot occasionally used the front office after hours but had to wash themselves in semi-darkness so that no one passing by in the street would see them. Electricity had to be used sparingly, because when their rations ran out, they were left without light or warmth. In that situation, they had to use candles to enable them to see, and pile coats on the beds at night to ward off the cold. When it was dark and they had no electricity, they amused themselves and kept warm by exercising and dancing. Illness was another cause for alarm because they could not call a doctor. In the winter of 1942, Anne had a high fever brought on by influenza, and all kinds of potions and remedies were used to cure her.

Being cramped in a few small rooms with no chance to escape affected them all. Squabbles broke out over minor matters, and relationships grew extremely strained. Most of the arguments were about food, but other things also caused trouble. Mr. and Mrs. van Pels had some furious fights about money, while Mrs. Frank and Mrs. van Pels argued endlessly about bringing up children. Mrs. van Pels and Anne also had numerous quarrels, usually over Anne's "cheekiness."

Despite the fear, the practical problems, and the frequent arguments, there were also many humorous moments in hiding. Hermann van Pels loved to tell jokes, and Anne and Peter enjoyed dressing up for a giggle in their parents' clothes—Anne in her father's suit, Peter in one of his mother's dresses. Any cause for celebration was welcomed in the annex. Birthdays, religious festivals, good news of the war, etc.—all were greeted with enormous pleasure. The helpers often joined in the celebrations, and even threw a surprise party in the annex at the end of 1942 to welcome in the New Year. Such occasions made life a little less dull.

Everyone in hiding tried to keep themselves as quietly busy as possible through the day: studying, sewing, writing, reading. To her annoyance, Anne wasn't always allowed to read the same books as Margot and Peter, but she loved biographies, mythology, and romance. She compiled family trees and studied shorthand with Margot and Peter. Mr. Frank made sure that the three teenagers didn't miss out on their education and tutored them in a variety of subjects, including languages, algebra, geometry, geography, and history. The attic became a peaceful spot for study. Anne also used it as a writing room, and Peter had made himself a carpentry workshop in one corner. After her lessons and at night, Anne sometimes relieved her boredom by borrowing her father's binoculars and zooming in on the houses opposite the courtyard. Past the black skeleton of the chestnut tree, she could see a dentist's office where the patient one evening was an elderly woman who was "awfully scared."

In her diary, Anne compared being in hiding to being on vacation in a very strange hotel. She tried to be brave, but at night fear often got the better of her, and the silence made her imagination run wild. The minutes crawled by, and each creak and movement made her wonder if they had been discovered. Planes flew past, firing at the enemy in the dark, and she felt sure that the annex would be hit by a bomb. Nighttime terrors aside, she often wrote about how lucky she felt to be in hiding with people she knew, cared for by friends. She only really became downhearted when she thought about her old life, her friends, and her cat, Moortje, whom she missed very much. She wrote then how miserable she was: "When someone comes in from the outside, with the wind in their clothes

and the cold air on their faces, then I could bury my head
in the blankets to stop myself thinking: When will we
be granted the privilege of smelling fresh air . . . ?
Cycling, dancing, whistling, looking out into the world,
feeling young, to know that I am free—that's what I long
for." She escaped into daydreams of "after the war," but
found that the best way to overcome her fears and sad-
ness was to go up into the attic where the window was
open. There she could gaze at the sky and the tower of
the Westerkerk. Staring at the chestnut tree, "on whose
branches little raindrops shone, at the seagulls and other
birds that looked like silver in the sun" brought her peace
for a while.

The helpers tried to protect their friends from the
reality of life on the outside, the deportations and the
cruelties, but it was impossible to keep everything secret.
Besides, the people in hiding wanted to know the truth,
however bad it was. They listened to the radio regularly
and heard reports on the Dutch station, Radio Oranje, of
Jews being killed by shooting and poisoned by gas. They
tried hard to keep their spirits up, despite the horror of
it all, by keeping to their routine and burying themselves
in work and hobbies. Anne wrote sensibly in her diary: "It
won't do us any good or help those outside to go on being
as gloomy as we are at the moment. . . . Must I keep
thinking about those people whatever I am doing and if
I want to laugh about something, should I stop myself

quickly and feel ashamed that I am cheerful? Ought I then to cry the whole day long? No, that I can't do."

The persecutions made them more aware than ever before of their Jewish identity. Of the eight in hiding, Pfeffer was the most religious, but they all observed the major festivals, enjoyed traditional Jewish food when it was available, and welcomed in the Sabbath every Friday night. Anne's interest in her religion increased as she got older. She had nightmares about the fate of other Jewish people, and in her dreams saw her friend Lies dressed in rags, starving and crying for help. For Anne, Lies became a symbol of Jewish persecution, and in her diary she wrote how guilty she felt to be sleeping in a warm bed while her friends were suffering: "I get frightened when I think of close friends who have now been delivered into the hands of the cruelest brutes the world has ever seen. And all because they are Jews."

Anne was frequently upset about other things, too, including her relationship with her mother. The two had many fights, which were largely the result of the pressures of being in hiding and Anne's need for independence (she felt that her mother treated her like a baby). Anne's father did his best to keep the peace between his wife and daughter, but in the end it was Anne herself who learned to have more patience with her mother and to try to see things from her viewpoint for a change.

Being in hiding did not prevent Anne from taking care

of her appearance and pride in it. She pin-curled her hair in the same style as Margot and made a combing-shawl out of rose-patterned material, which she tied under her chin to catch stray hairs when she brushed out her curls. She dreamed of being able to buy lots of makeup and clothes after the war, writing out in her diary a long list of what she thought she would need. In the mirror, she studied her face and asked Margot whether she was attractive. (Margot told her she had nice eyes!) From time to time, everyone tried to make a real fuss over her; the helpers brought her new shoes and the cinema magazines they knew she loved to spoil her a bit. They knew that it was very difficult for a lively and sociable young girl to put up with the quiet and loneliness of life in hiding. In early 1944, she noticed that Peter was becoming more interested in her, and when he looked at her she was happy and excited. Soon he was confiding in her, which was exactly what she wanted. They spent hours in the attic together, sitting by the window and looking out at the Westerkerk or across the courtyard and watching winter turn to spring on the chestnut tree. However, the intense feelings Anne had for Peter gradually began to fade; he could not satisfy her need to talk about "deeper" subjects, and he wasn't as intelligent as she was.

In 1944, Anne wrote at length in her diary about how she had changed since her birthday in 1942. She now felt that she was a young woman, one who wanted something different from the lives led by other women she knew, something more than a husband and family (although she wanted those, too): "Although I'm only fourteen, I know quite well what I want, I know who is right and who is wrong, I have my opinions, my own ideas and principles, and although it may sound pretty mad from an adolescent, I feel more of a person than a child, I feel quite independent of anyone." She sometimes found it hard to be optimistic, but with a struggle, she succeeded: "It's really a wonder I haven't dropped all my ideals, because they seem so absurd and impossible to carry out. Yet I keep them because, in spite of everything, I still believe that people are really good at heart."

When the deportations began, rumors about the "work camps for Jews" started to spread. In leaflets written by resistance organizations, attention was drawn to the gassings in Poland, and the BBC Home Service—which Anne listened to from her hiding place—carried reports of Jews being "regularly killed by machine gun fire, hand grenades—and even poisoned by gas." Most people did not believe these reports. But many of those who did, and who were appalled by what was happening, decided to resist.

Like the people whom they hid, all the rescuers were different: They were rich and poor, religious and atheist, with families and without. Some saved those whom they knew, others saved strangers. Their common bond was the courage to act, in the knowledge that the punishment they faced was imprisonment, deportation, or death.

What motivated them? Marion Pritchard, a rescuer in Holland, explains: "One morning on my way to school I passed a small Jewish children's home. The Germans were loading the children, who ranged in age from babies to eight year olds, on to trucks. They were upset and crying. When they did not move fast enough, the Nazis picked them up by an arm, a leg, the hair, and threw them into the trucks. To watch grown-up men treat small children that way—I could not believe my eyes. I found myself literally crying with rage. Two women coming down the street tried to interfere physically. The Germans heaved them into the truck too. I just sat there on my bicycle, and that was the moment I decided that is there was anything I could do to thwart such atrocities I would do it."

Apart from all practical matters such as providing a hiding place, food, warmth, and security, helpers had to be supportive to the people whom they hid, who often didn't see anyone else other than their rescuers. Miep Gies recalls: "I never felt the desire to be free of the Frank family. It was my fate, my burden, and my duty." In an interview, when asked if she was ever afraid, Miep replied, "No, especially not at the beginning . . . caring for those people was the main thing. Sometimes I lay awake at night and thought, 'Oh those poor people hidden up there, how awful. How would I feel?' . . . We, the helpers, were aware that occasionally there were difficult moments for each one of us, but we didn't talk about it. Everything had to take its course, and if you were to talk about it, you'd begin to feel a certain pressure. You'd spend the day thinking about the people in hiding, and that couldn't happen. We had to appear as relaxed as possible to the rest of the world, otherwise people would become suspicious."

In her diary, Anne Frank pays tribute not only to Miep and the other people who hid her family, but to all rescuers: "It is amazing how much noble, unselfish work these people are doing risking their own lives to help and save others. Our helpers are a very good example. . . . Never have we heard *one* word of the burden which we must certainly be to them, never has one of them complained of all the trouble we give. They all come upstairs every day, talk to the men about business and politics, to the women about food and wartime difficulties, and about newspapers and books with the children. They put on the brightest possible faces, bring flowers and presents for birthdays and bank holidays, are always ready to help and do all they can. That is something we must never forget; although others may show their heroism in the war or against the Germans, our helpers display heroism in their cheerfulness and affection."

Although most helpers worked alone, there were also whole communities who came together to save Jews from

Miep Gies

deportation. In Denmark, when the Germans announced their plans to deport all Jews, the king and the heads of the Danish churches objected, and Danish universities shut down so that students could help in the rescue effort. The deportations were due to take place on the night of October 1, 1943. The population, forewarned, moved into action, and 7,220 Jews and 680 non-Jewish family members were taken to ports where Danish sea captains and fishermen took them onto their boats and sailed them to safety in neutral Sweden. The Germans, enraged, started to hunt for Jews who had been too old or sick to travel; they found 500 and sent them straight to Theresienstadt. But still Denmark did not forget: Every month, the Danish authorities asked for an update on these Jews' condition and insisted they must not be harmed. Aware that they were being watched, the Nazis did not abuse them. Of the 500 Jews from Denmark who had been deported, 423 survived the war.

One of the most famous cases of "desk rescue" comes from Hungary. After the Nazi invasion of Hungary in 1944, Raoul Wallenberg, a thirty-two-year-old Swedish banker, issued 630 Swedish visas to Hungarian Jews, and his colleague, Charles Lutz, issued 700. Working on behalf of the American-based War Refugee Board, Wallenberg was also able to give homes to 15,000 Jews in a number of apartments funded by the Board. The passes he had issued gave the Jews protection by the Swedish government. The

Nazis were furious and arrested 80,000 Hungarian Jews in Budapest. They were marched into Austria under conditions so terrible that almost half of them died. Wallenberg followed the survivors and gave out protective passes so that they could return home. In the meantime, orders had been given for the 70,000 Jews living in the Budapest ghetto without passes to be killed. Wallenberg contacted the SS general in charge of the executions and told him that he would be hung as a war criminal if the murders went ahead. The SS man decided not to carry out the order. Wallenberg continued to help Jews until January of 1945, when Russian troops entered Budapest. He was last seen driving to the Russian commander's headquarters to discuss saving the city's remaining Jews. He was arrested by Russian soldiers and imprisoned in Moscow on suspicion of spying for the Americans. Wallenberg was never heard from again.

In Kovno, where more than 30,000 Jews had lived before the war, two hundred children were saved by Lithuanians who hid them in the city and surrounding countryside. A twelve-year-old orphan called Sima led Jews out of the Minsk ghetto into the Russian forests. Her youth, blonde hair, wide blue eyes, and sweet face prevented the Nazis from suspecting her. A resistance fighter who worked with Sima recalls: "No assignment was too difficult for Sima. Before going out on a mission she listened carefully to the given instruction, then she would repeat what she was told, trying hard not to miss a single word. Her small pistol was always in the special pocket sewn into her coat. Before starting out she would always point at it and say, 'Don't worry, the Fritzes [Germans] will not take me alive.'" Sima survived the war.

Even some young Germans were determined to speak out against the Nazis. Hans and Sophie Scholl, a brother and sister in a large, politically active family who despised Hitler, didn't hide Jews but were disgusted by what was happening to them. Hans and Sophie attended Munich University where, together with a small group of friends, they formed the White Rose resistance group. Their methods were pacifist: They wrote and distributed leaflets urging people to take a stand against the Nazis, and especially against the anti-Jewish measures. Soon their actions came to the attention of the Nazis themselves, who became determined to find the leaders of the White Rose group.

On February 18, 1943, Hans and Sophie started distributing the latest White Rose leaflet, in which they had written of their delight about the German defeat in Russia. The university caretaker saw them and had them arrested. Sophie and Hans were taken to the Gestapo headquarters in Munich. They refused to betray anyone, but other members of the group were soon arrested. Hans and Sophie's parents tried desperately to secure their release, but the Scholls and one other member of the White Rose, Christoph Probst, were sentenced to death. Their parents visited them in jail before they were executed. When Mrs. Scholl began to weep, Sophie told her brightly, "It's only a few years' more life I'll miss!" That evening, Hans and Sophie were killed by guillotine. As Hans walked to his death he shouted, "Long live freedom!" Other members of the White Rose were also executed. A few days after Sophie and Hans's burial in south Munich, graffiti appeared on walls throughout the town. It read: "Their spirit lives."

Despite the severe limitations on their own personal freedom, many Jews were also active in the resistance. In 1943, the Nazis announced their plans to deport the remaining inhabitants of the Warsaw ghetto. On the morning of April 19, German soldiers entering the ghetto were attacked by gunfire and grenades made from gasoline-filled bottles. Stunned that the Jews were fighting back, the soldiers immediately retreated. The following day they returned and broke into the Jewish hospital, where they shot all the patients before setting fire to the building. Despite this, ghetto fighters continued to attack Nazi soldiers entering the compound for nearly an entire month. The ghetto fighters had just two machine guns and fifteen rifles; the Nazis had 135 machine guns and 1,358 rifles.

In the end, the Nazis set fire to the ghetto. Seven thousand Jews were killed; fifty-six thousand captured. Those who had been captured were either killed immediately or sent to death camps. Four months later, on August 1, when Polish forces fought against the German occupiers, those Jews who had managed to survive the ghetto emerged again to do battle with their enemies. The Germans brought the uprising to an end on October 2. A few Jews found new hiding places in the rubble of the destroyed city.

Jewish resistance occurred in every country on some level; for instance, in Holland, a group of Jews calling themselves the Palestine Pioneers helped people to escape the country. Their headquarters was a farm near the village of Loosdrecht where one of the organizers, a non-Jew named Joop Westerweel, worked with a German Jewish refugee, Joachim Simon. Most of the people whom they rescued were able to reach Palestine, but both Westerweel and Simon were captured by the SS and executed.

One of the most famous cases of Jewish women's resistance is that of Hannah Senesh, who was born in Budapest, Hungary, in 1921. Hannah's father was a playwright, and both her parents were interested in politics and culture. She never thought about what it meant to be Jewish until she experienced discrimination at school. Afterward, she became a committed Zionist and left Budapest for Palestine in September 1939. Hannah volunteered to serve in the British military during the war and was parachuted into Yugoslavia on a secret mission. As she crossed the border into Hungary, she was captured by Nazis, who imprisoned her in her hometown.

Hannah Senesh

She was twenty-three years old when she was killed by firing squad. Shortly before she was put to death, she wrote a poem in her prison cell:

> One—two—three . . .
> Eight feet long,
> Two strides across, the rest is dark . . .
> Life hangs over me like a question mark.
> One—two—three . . .
> Maybe another week,
> Or next month, may still find me here,
> But death, I feel, is very near.
>
> I could have been
> Twenty-three next July;
> I gambled on what mattered most,
> The dice were cast. I lost."

Budapest, 1944

Despite the efforts of rescuers and resistance workers—many more than are mentioned here—a large number of those who went into hiding were betrayed. In Holland, the *Police Gazette* published lists of Jews who were missing, calling for their capture. The Nazis tried to fool Jews in hiding by taking out a public notice telling them to give themselves up and promising that they would not be deported. It was a lie. The Nazis also employed people to hunt out Jews, and offered money to anyone who could tell them where Jews were hiding. In Holland, there was an infamous group of men called the Henneicke Column who captured hundreds of Jews. At first their wages were low, but as time went on and fewer Jews were found (most of them having been deported), betrayers were given a pay raise to encourage them to work harder.

Some people who were not actually employed by the Nazis to betray Jews did so anyway, and had different reasons for making phone calls or writing letters to the authorities about hidden Jews. Some were anti-Semitic or had a personal grudge against a particular Jewish person, while others acted out of malice, or because they thought they should obey the law. In Holland, approximately 9,000 of the 25,000 Jews who went into hiding were arrested due to informants. Their hiding places were ransacked by the Nazis, who took out anything of value either to keep for themselves or to send back to Germany.

Discovery was never very far away. Every month during 1942 and 1943, 12,000 Jews were deported from Holland. They included those who had been betrayed in hiding and those who were taken in the mass roundups. On January 20, 1943, a train left Holland for Auschwitz carrying over a thousand Jewish adults from the Apeldoorn home for the mentally ill, and 74 boys and 24 girls from the nearby home for seriously physically and mentally handicapped children. With the children were the nurses who had always cared for them; they had been told that they could stay with their patients or start new jobs in a very modern home for the mentally ill "in the east." The nurses chose to stay with the children. Upon arrival at Auschwitz, everyone on board the train was sent straight to the gas chambers.

The last large-scale raid in Amsterdam took place on September 29, 1943. Approximately 5,000 Jews were arrested. Afterward, the only Jews still living in Holland were those married to non-Jews, those with fake identity papers, and those who were in hiding.

Anne's diary was a great comfort to her, just as she had hoped it would be. She usually wrote in it in her parents' room, in her own room, or at a desk by the window in the attic. Everyone in hiding knew that Anne was keeping a diary, because she often asked them not to disturb her while she was writing, and she sometimes read aloud from it, though no one ever tried to read it without her permission. When the original diary her father had bought her was full, the helpers gave her office ledgers and sheets of loose paper to write on. In the summer of 1943, Anne began to write short stories. Some of these, such as "The Battle of the Potatoes" and "Villains!" were essays about the daily routine in the annex. "Villains!" concerned the problem of fleas in the annex during the summer months, although the villains were not the fleas, but the van Pelses, who had ignored the advice they had been given about how to get rid of the tiny pests, resulting in an outbreak of itchiness. Other stories, such as "Kitty" and "Eva's Dream," were more like fairy tales. Anne kept a record of all her non-diary work in an oblong office cashbook, providing an index and details of when the stories were written. Sometimes she read aloud from this book to her companions and the helpers.

At the start of 1944, Anne was already thinking about what would happen to her diary after the war: "I trust to luck, but should I be saved, and spared from destruction, then it would be terrible if my diaries and tales were lost." Her writing, she felt, was the finest thing she had, and she now knew what she wanted to do when the war was over and she had completed her education: "I want to write later on, and even if I don't become a writer I won't neglect my writing while doing some other job. Oh yes, I don't want to have lived for nothing like most people. I want to go on living after my death! And therefore I am grateful to God for giving me this gift, this possibility of developing myself and of writing, of expressing all that is in me."

On March 28, 1944, Anne was listening to Radio Oranje, broadcast from London. A speech by the Dutch Minister for Education, Art, and Science urged people to keep all their personal documents, such as diaries and letters, safe. When the war was over, these would then be kept in a special center so that future generations could learn how ordinary people had lived. The other occupants of the secret annex immediately turned to Anne and began talking excitedly about her diary. Anne herself was thrilled by the idea and began rewriting her whole diary with a view to publication. On May 11, she started work properly on the task of adapting her diary into a book she wanted to call "Het Achterhuis" ("The House Behind"). The new version was written on sheets of colored carbon paper. Anne altered parts of what she had originally written, deleted some details, added others, and combined a number of entries. She drew up a list of name changes for everyone she had mentioned, calling herself "Anne Robin." On June 12, 1944, Anne turned fifteen, and as a present, Miep and Bep gave her a collection of unused office ledgers in which to write. Anne then asked Bep about the possibility of sending her stories off to magazines under another name. When Bep asked her if she really wanted to be a writer, she said, "Yes . . . no . . . yes . . ." then answered with a sudden, brilliant smile, "No, I want to marry early and have lots of children!"

Two months later, on August 1, Anne wrote her last letter to Kitty, the name she had given to her diary. She ended it ". . . if I'm quiet and serious, everyone thinks it's a new comedy and then I have to get out of it by turning it into a joke, not to mention my own family, who are sure to think I'm ill, make me swallow pills for headaches and nerves, feel my neck and my head to see whether I'm running a temperature, ask me if I'm constipated and criticize me for being in a bad mood. I can't keep that up: if I'm watched to that extent, I start by getting snappy, then unhappy, and finally I twist my heart around again so that the bad is on the outside and the good is on the inside, and keep on trying to find a way of becoming what I would so like to be and what I could be, if . . . there weren't any other people living in the world. Yours, Anne M. Frank."

Early on the morning of August 4, 1944, a telephone call was made to the Gestapo headquarters in south Amsterdam. The caller told officials that there were eight Jews in hiding at 263 Prinsengracht. At ten thirty that same day, four members of the Gestapo raided the secret annex.

EIGHT:

"I AM AFRAID OF PRISON CELLS AND CONCENTRATION CAMPS . . ."

Whether they were discovered in hiding or picked up during one of the mass raids, Jews were usually sent first to a transit camp in the country of their capture. The transit camps were miniature concentration camps without gas chambers. They were in remote areas, away from major towns or villages, surrounded by high barbed-wire fencing and patrolled by armed guards.

Upon arrival, newcomers were registered and made to hand over their possessions. They were then searched for hidden valuables and told which barracks they would be in. Most transit camps let families stay together during the day, but at night men and women were separated. There were daily roll calls (*Appell*) to check the number of inmates, and forced labor for everyone except the very sick, the very old, or the very young. At mealtimes, prisoners formed a long, weary line for a bowl of watery soup and hard bread. In the French transit camp Rivesaltes, children were starving. Those who could still walk had to line up for their poor rations. Children, huddled in filthy gray blankets and rags, lined up on the rocky ground holding rusty cans they used for bowls, their hands outstretched for scraps of food.

There was no privacy in the transit camps. Toilet and wash facilities were few and filthy. At night, people slept on wooden bunks without blankets or mattresses in barracks that were freezing and often without electricity. Under such conditions, most prisoners became ill with exhaustion, hunger, or disease. Family life became almost impossible, but children and their parents did their best to stay together and provide support for one another. In some transit camps, there were very basic schools for the children left behind in the barracks while their parents went to work. There were no textbooks and few writing materials. Lessons were given mostly by speech alone, and children had to listen and remember what they had learned. Classes never stayed the same from one week to the next because most of the teachers and their pupils eventually ended up being deported.

In France, rumors of what was happening to the Jews led a group of humanitarian organizations including Oeuvre de Secours aux Enfants (OSE) and the Fédération des Societés Juives en France to try to convince the authorities to release some of the children from the transit camps. In the summer of 1942, a number of children *were* handed over to the OSE workers. The moment of separation from their parents was very hard. Although parents knew and were glad that their children were being saved, they could hardly bear to let their sons and daughters go. The scenes of departure were heart-rending. Very young children had no idea why they were being separated from their parents and screamed to be allowed to return to them as they were lined up for the buses that would take them out of the camp. The older children, who understood something of the pain their parents felt, tried to be brave and held back their tears. As the buses drove off, weeping mothers clung to the doors.

In July 1942, 13,000 Jews were captured in Paris, among them 4,000 children. The children were sent, without their parents, to Drancy transit camp in a suburb of Paris. Within two weeks, the children had been deported. An eyewitness recalled watching as the children were awakened at five o'clock in the morning and made to dress in the half-light. It was cold, and the youngest children cried to go back to their bunks. The gendarmes picked up those who refused to get out of bed and dress, and dragged them down to the yard to wait as their names were called out. Confused with sleepiness and fear, many of the children did not answer or responded to the wrong name. The older children tried to comfort the little ones as best they could. In the end, none of the children survived the war.

In 1944, a group of Jewish children arrived in Drancy from an orphanage in the village of Izieu. Teacher Miron Zlatin had taken forty-four Jewish children into the orphanage where he worked and told no one, other than his staff, that the children were Jewish, and not actually orphans. The youngest child was four, the eldest was seventeen. They were well cared for by the staff and formed close friendships with the other children. One of the hidden children, eleven-year-old Liliane Gerenstein, who was staying at the orphanage with her little brother, wrote a letter to God, which has survived: "God? It is thanks to You that I had a beautiful life before, that I was spoiled, that I had lovely things that others do not have. God? After that I ask You one thing only: Make my parents come back. My poor parents, protect them (even more than You protect me) so that I can see them again as soon as possible. Make them come back again. . . . I had such a good mother and such a good father! I have such faith in You and I thank You in advance."

Along with all the other Jewish children, Liliane and her brother were caught by the Nazis in April of 1944, when SS soldiers raided the orphanage looking for hidden children. They were sent first to Drancy, then to Auschwitz.

Miron Zlatin and two of the children ended up in another camp, where they were murdered. In Auschwitz, one of the teachers, Léa Feldblum, begged the Nazis to let the children go; she told the soldiers on the platform in the camp that the children were from an orphanage, hoping this might change their minds. The SS sent her alone into the camp, then marched the other five teachers and all the children to the gas chambers. Léa Feldblum survived the war.

In Czechoslovakia, the ghetto Theresienstadt served as a transit camp for Auschwitz. When the Red Cross wanted to visit Theresienstadt to see how Jews were being treated, the Nazis told them that it was a town given to the Jews by Hitler, mostly inhabited by families of men who had fought for Germany during the First World War. In fact, it was no different from any of the other transit camps, apart from its active artistic community. Children put on musicals and plays, created their own newspaper, wrote stories, and painted. The best known artist to emerge from Theresienstadt is probably Helga Weissova-Hoskova, who arrived in the camp after being taken, at the age of twelve, from her hometown of Prague in December of 1941. She kept a diary of ghetto life in a series of beautiful paintings. Together with her mother, Helga survived Theresienstadt, Auschwitz, and Mathausen, and today she is a successful artist.

Jewish painter Friedl Dicker-Brandeis was also imprisoned in Theresienstadt, where she encouraged children to express their emotions through art. She brought her crayons, paper, and paints with her into the ghetto and taught children about color and creativity. Ela Weissberger was one of those whom Friedl Dicker-Brandeis taught. She remembers: "Before Brandeis, we were all just sitting there waiting for the next horrible thing to happen. Can you imagine being in a Nazi camp with nothing to do? Brandeis let a lot of light in where there was darkness." Another girl, twelve-year-old Alice Guttmanova, drew the deportation train with crayons shortly before being sent to Auschwitz, where she was gassed in 1943. Friedl Dicker-Brandeis kept all the artwork in two suitcases. When she heard that she, too, was going to be deported to Auschwitz in October of 1944, she buried the suitcases behind a brick wall, hoping someone would find them after the war. She did not survive, but when the war ended and building work began in the city, workers found the suitcases. The artwork was recently exhibited in the United States, where it was seen by thousands of people.

Of 15,000 children imprisoned in Theresienstadt, only 1,100 survived the war.

August 4, 1944, was a warm, still summer's day in Amsterdam. By mid-morning, everyone in the secret annex was in their usual place, reading or studying quietly. In the offices below, Miep, Bep, Kugler, and Kleiman were busy with routine tasks, and on the ground floor, the warehousemen were mixing and packing spices. At about ten thirty A.M., a car pulled up in front of the building. Several men got out. One of them asked the warehouseman standing at the door a question. He pointed upstairs, and the men went inside.

In the front office, Miep, Bep, and Kleiman all looked up as the door opened, having heard footsteps on the stairs. A man stood before them, not in uniform, but holding a gun. "Don't move," he said. "Just sit there quietly and don't move." He went through to the next office, leaving the three of them sitting there motionless, in utter shock. Miep suddenly said, "Bep, we've had it."

In the office next door, Kugler heard footsteps in the corridor and then his door, too, opened. He started at the sight of the men before him. Several Dutch Nazis stood in the doorway, all in ordinary clothes apart from their leader, Karl Josef Silberbauer, who wore the uniform of the Gestapo. He asked Kugler who was in charge of the offices.

"I am," Kugler replied.

One of the other men stepped forward. "We know everything," he said. "You're hiding Jews and they're in this building. Take us to them."

Kugler felt the blood rush to his face. He knew it was over. He got up and led the way upstairs.

In the front office, Miep searched her bag for the illegal ration cards needed to feed eight people in hiding. She held them in her lap as she dipped into her bag again, taking out money and her husband Jan's lunch. When Jan arrived a short while later, the Gestapo were still in the building. Miep was able to stop him at the office door. She handed him his lunch, and then the money and ration cards for safekeeping, whispering urgently, "It's wrong here." He understood and left the building.

Upstairs, Kugler and the Nazis had reached the corridor where the bookcase hid the entrance to the secret annex. Kugler pretended that there was nothing else to see, but the Nazis shook the bookcase until they found the hook holding it against the wall. They lifted it from its latch, and the door to the secret annex was revealed. Silberbauer drew his gun. He pushed Kugler in front, his pistol pressed against his spine, and ordered softly: "In."

Kugler walked slowly along the corridor to the left of the staircase. It was unpleasantly humid, as it always was during the summer months. In the Franks' sitting room, Anne's mother was standing alone, beside the table. She looked anxious and confused by Kugler's unexpected appearance. With a great effort, Kugler said, "The Gestapo are here."

Downstairs, one of the Dutch Nazis strode into the office, where Bep, Miep, and Kleiman were still waiting. He told Kleiman to accompany him into Kugler's office. After ten minutes, Kleiman reappeared alone, having been ordered to hand the keys of the building over to Miep. He gave Bep his wallet and told her to take it to a friend, who had a pharmacy nearby. "Tell him to pass it on to my wife," Kleiman said, hoping that at least one of them could

The office personnel in Otto Frank's company, from left to right:
Victor Kugler, Esther, Bep Voskuyl, Pine, and Miep Gies.

escape. Bep ran out of the building, unseen. Before returning to the back office, Kleiman pressed the keys into Miep's palm and whispered, "See that you stay out of this, Miep. You can't save us, but make the best of a bad thing here."

Miep nodded, speechless.

Upstairs in the annex, the Nazis now entered the other secret rooms, rounding everyone up. Mr. Frank and Peter were the last to know they had been discovered. They were studying English in Peter's room when they heard someone racing up the stairs. Mr. Frank jumped to his feet, astonished. The door flew open and a man pointed a pistol straight at them: "Raise your hands." Neither of them said anything; the shock was too great. They followed the man into the van Pelses' room, where Mr. and Mrs. van Pels and Fritz Pfeffer stood with their hands above their heads. Another Nazi ordered them downstairs to the first floor of the annex.

Anne stood silently with her mother and sister in the middle of their living room, hands raised. Margot wept softly. Kugler was there, too. The sun glittered through the thick curtains. Silberbauer turned to Anne's father and asked, "Where are your valuables?"

Mr. Frank pointed to a small cupboard. Silberbauer lifted out a small cashbox containing a few pieces of jewelry and some money. He glanced about and his gaze fell on Mr. Frank's briefcase. He picked it up and shook it open.

Notebooks, loose papers, and a checked-covered auto-graph album fell out: Anne's diary. Anne said nothing. Silberbauer emptied the cashbox into the briefcase, along with a few other objects. "Have you any weapons?" he asked, snapping the briefcase shut.

They all shook their heads.

"Good," Silberbauer said. "Now get ready. I want every-one back here in five minutes."

It did not take long for them to pack their small "emergency" bags, which they had always intended to use if a bomb fell near the annex and they needed to escape in a hurry. While everyone was doing that, Silberbauer paced about the room. "How long have you been here?" he asked Anne's father.

When Mr. Frank told him it was just over two years, Silberbauer looked amazed. *Two years?* he said. "I don't believe you."

Anne's father showed him some pencil marks on one wall, along with letters and dates and said, "That's where we've measured the height of my youngest daughter while we've been here."

Silberbauer was further surprised when Mr. Frank told him he had been a lieutenant in the German army during the First World War. His manner changed slightly after that. He told everyone that they could take their time packing their things and told his men to allow them some space to do this. Later, Mr. Frank recalled, "Anne walked back and forth, and did not even glance at her diary. Perhaps she had a premonition that all was lost now."

When they had all gathered their belongings, Silberbauer ordered them along the corridor to the swinging bookcase. When they were all in the hallway, one of the Nazis locked the door and shoved the bookcase into place.

Alone in her office, Miep heard them coming down the wooden staircase "like beaten dogs."

They gathered in the private office and stood there silently. Silberbauer fired questions, first at Kugler, then at Kleiman. Their answer was always: "I have nothing to say."

"All right," Silberbauer snapped, his color rising. "Then you'll come along too."

A group of curious onlookers had gathered near the waiting police van in front of the warehouse. Among them was Jan Gies with Kleiman's brother, and the warehouse clerks. The ten prisoners—the Franks, the van Pelses, Pfeffer, and Kleiman and Kugler—climbed into the van. The bells of the Westerkerk rang out. Then the doors slammed shut, and darkness fell around them.

Following their arrest, the Franks, the van Pelses, Pfeffer, Kugler, and Kleiman were taken to the Gestapo headquarters in south Amsterdam. In the courtyard, a black flag with the emblem of the SS flew from a tall white pole.

The offices were in a large, redbrick former school. The ten prisoners were led into this building and locked in a room with several other prisoners. They seemed numbed. Anne, Margot, and Peter occasionally whispered to one another. Mr. Frank turned to Kleiman and said in a low voice, "You can't imagine how I feel. To think that you are sitting here among us, that we are to blame—"

"Don't give it another thought," said Kleiman. "It was up to me and I wouldn't have done it any differently."

After a while, Kugler and Kleiman were taken to another cell. Apart from Otto Frank, they never saw their friends again.

The Franks, the van Pelses, and Pfeffer were taken into Silberbauer's office for questioning. Mr. Frank was asked if he knew where other Jews were hiding. He replied that he didn't; having been in hiding himself for two years, he had lost touch with everyone. Silberbauer believed him. The prisoners returned to their cells for the night but were transferred the following day to the Weteringschans jail in the center of Amsterdam. It was a huge, ugly building with two wings extending out from a center block, overlooking a filthy stretch of canal. Metal bars were at the windows. The Franks, the van Pelses, and Pfeffer remained there for two days.

On August 8, four days after their arrest, the Franks and their friends were taken to Amsterdam's Centraal Station. The train that arrived to take them out of the city looked like an ordinary one, but as soon as the passengers climbed aboard, the doors were locked and bolted behind them. Despite this, they were hopeful for the future, since by now it was clear that the Germans were losing the war. Anne stayed by the window throughout the journey, spellbound by the countryside. For a short while, it was almost like freedom, but by late afternoon, the train had reached its destination: Kamp Westerbork.

Westerbork was in Drenthe, eighty miles north of Amsterdam, and in a very lonely spot. Before the war it had been a refugee camp for German Jews, set up by the Dutch government. When war broke out, the refugees were evacuated so that the Germans could redesign the camp. The refugees returned when it was completed, now as a transit camp. A high barbed-wire fence surrounded 107 wooden barracks, each containing three-tier bunks—enough to house three hundred people. Work began at five o'clock in the morning for the inmates, who had to take apart old airplane batteries while the guards watched over them. The commandant of Westerbork, Alfred Gemmeker, lived in a house on the edge of the camp and ran a small chicken farm.

Irene Butter-Hasenberg was twelve years old when she arrived in Westerbork. Her first impression was how dark it was that night; soon she was in a line, waiting to be checked for head lice, then undressing with hundreds of other strangers as doctors examined everyone. Men and women were separated, and those who were found to have lice had their heads shaved. Irene did not have lice, but she was afraid that she would catch them and lose her hair. She looked at the newly bald inmates, and with horror realized she didn't recognize any of them without their hair. Despite her experience in the camps, Irene survived the war.

Eva Geiringer was also sent to the camp. Her feelings upon arrival were different from those of Irene: "We hadn't been especially afraid of going to Westerbork. It wasn't a concentration camp and we thought we might stay there until the liberation. I was very happy to be with my father and brother again. . . . We had begun to be really hopeful again. We never thought that we wouldn't survive." But each week, a list was made of those who would be deported from Westerbork, either to Sobibor or Auschwitz. To their horror, one evening, Eva and her family heard their names read out: "We tried everything we could to change things, but it was no good. The people who compiled the list were mainly Jews, I think, and they did what they could to protect their friends and relatives. But for the rest, well, we just had to go. Everyone packed what they had, though later they took it all from us."

When the Franks, the van Pelses, and Pfeffer arrived at Westerbork on the afternoon of August 8, they went through the usual routine for new arrivals. They were sent first to the registration desks in the main square. Ration cards were handed over, then personal information entered on forms and cards. The woman who took down the Franks' details was a Jewish prisoner, Vera Cohn. She recalled: "Mr. Frank was a pleasant looking man, courteous and cultured. He stood before me tall and straight. He answered my routine questions quietly. Anne was by his side. Her face, by certain standards, was not a pretty one, but her eyes—bright, young, eager eyes—made you look at her again. She was fifteen then . . . none of the Franks showed any signs of despair over their plight. . . . Their composure, as they grouped around my typing desk in the receiving room, was one of quiet dignity."

Before being led to their barracks, all newcomers were asked if they had any valuables with them. They were thoroughly searched, then sent to their barracks. Because they had been in hiding, the Franks and their friends were "convict Jews," which meant that they were held in the punishment compound, Barrack 67. Their freedom was limited even by the standards of the camp. Instead of keeping their own clothes, they were given blue overalls with red shoulder patches, and wooden clogs. Men had their heads shaved, and women had their hair cropped. They were not allowed any soap, and they received less food than the other prisoners, even though their work was harder.

On their first day in the camp, the Franks met Mr. and Mrs. de Winter and their daughter Judy, who was the same age as Anne. The de Winters had been in hiding for over a year when a spy betrayed them to the Gestapo. They became close to the Franks in Westerbork. Each day they all attended roll call before work began at five o'clock in the morning. Children were sent to the cable workshop and adults to the industrial department where they spent the day taking apart old airplane batteries at long tables. They could talk to one another, but guards stood over them while they worked, yelling at them to speed up. Lunch was stale bread and watery soup. Working alongside the Franks were two sisters, Janny and Lientje Brilleslijper. Lientje recalled, "The two girls, Margot and Anne, were very attached to their mother. Anne wrote in her diary that her mother didn't understand her, but I think that was just an adolescent mood. She clung to her mother in the camp."

Also in the punishment block was Rachel van Amerongen–Frankfoorder. Rachel worked for Westerbork's internal service and Mr. Frank asked her if she could find another job for Anne. Rachel knew he was eager to do anything that might make life in the camp a little easier for her. Anne said, "I can do everything—I'm very handy," but there was nothing Rachel could do—she wasn't in charge.

Mrs. de Winter noticed the closeness between Mr. Frank and his younger daughter: "Anne's father was quiet . . . but it was a reassuring quietness that helped Anne and helped the rest of us too. He lived in the men's barracks, but once when Anne was sick, he came over to visit her every evening and would stand beside her bed for hours, telling her stories. Anne was so like him that when she recovered and David, a twelve-year-old boy who lived in the women's barracks, fell ill, she acted in just the same way, stood by his bed and talked to him. David came from an Orthodox family and he and Anne always talked about God."

In his memoir, Mr. Frank recalled: "At the camp we had to work, although we had the evenings off and we could be together. It was a particular relief for the children to no longer be locked away and to be able to talk with other people. We, the older ones, however, feared the danger of being transported to the rumored death camps of Poland. . . ."

At the beginning of September, the man in charge of Westerbork, Alfred Gemmeker, called the section leaders to his office and told them to put together a new list for deportation. The train was due to leave on the morning of September 3, 1944. The night before, one of the section leaders and an official entered the punishment barracks to read out the names on the list. Among the names were those of Herman, Auguste, and Peter van Pels, Fritz Pfeffer, Otto, Edith, Margot, and Anne Frank . . .

What was it like on board the deportation train? Rabbi Hugo Gryn was deported from Hungary in 1944, at the age of thirteen. He recalled his journey on the train to the concentration camp: "By noon inside the wagon [train] it was unbearably hot and the bucket [used as a toilet] in the box stunk to high heaven. There was plenty of food (hardly anyone ate), but the water barrel was nearly exhausted and the little water that was still in it was warm and full of dirt. The mountains were left behind and gradually the whole scenery changed. . . . The names of the stations were spelled in a different way and German soldiers were more frequent. We were in Poland! I sat down. There was not room for everyone, so we had to sit between each other's legs. Gabby in front of me [his brother] and Dad behind. We were not talking. The train raced with time itself and I was beginning to go mad. The heat, the thirst, the dirt—everything seemed to conspire against me."

Sherry Weiss-Rosenfeld was fifteen years old when she was sent to Auschwitz with her aunt and uncle in May 1944. Her journey was an unimaginable nightmare, with people packed into the train compartments until it was impossible to even turn around. One night there was a storm and the rain poured in through the wooden slats, bringing relief to everyone because there was no water on board for them to drink.

Conditions inside the train were so terrible that it seemed impossible to imagine anything worse. But that was until the trains arrived at their destination, and the doors opened.

Mrs. de Winter remembered: "On September 2, we were told that a thousand people would leave in the morning. . . . During the night we packed up the few things we had been allowed to keep. Someone had a little ink, and with that we marked our names on the blankets we were to take with us and we made the children repeat again and again the addresses where we were to meet after the war, in case we separated. I gave Judy the address of her aunt in Zutphen, and the Franks had agreed on an address in Switzerland."

As the sun rose on September 3, the main street of the camp was being closed off. The train itself had already arrived, a long chain of trucks that had rolled quietly into the camp during the night. On the platform stood Alfred Gemmeker with his dog at his side. Guards strolled about, relaxed and smiling. At seven o'clock that morning, men, women, and children began filing out of the barracks. Each passenger carried a backpack and a rolled-up blanket. They were instructed to walk forward in groups of three.

The sick and disabled were guided through on stretchers and carts. It was a high step from platform to train and a long wait until the carriages were filled. As doors closed, people put their hands through the gaps in the wooden slats. There were no windows in the train; these were the dreaded cattle trucks—dark, airless, and unbearably claustrophobic.

At eleven o'clock, the whistle blew. The guards still standing on the platform could read the inscription on the back of the train as it pulled away: "Westerbork—Auschwitz: Auschwitz—Westerbork. Do not uncouple the carriages, the entire train must return to Westerbork intact." The ninety-third transport from Westerbork contained 1,019 people (498 women, 442 men, and 79 children).

It was the very last train to leave Holland for Auschwitz.

Anne and her family and the friends they had made in Westerbork sat together on their backpacks, pressing themselves against the walls. They shared their car with the desperately sick. It was cramped—seventy-five people were packed tightly together—and became cold as they traveled by night. Straw lay on the floor, and there was a small bucket filled with drinking water. A larger bucket served as a toilet, and next to it lay a sandbag to soak up any spillage. A small lantern swung from the ceiling. It smelled terrible, and later the stench became worse when people had to use the toilet bucket and the weak began to die.

Hours passed and they knew they were in Germany. Whenever the train stopped, a guard would open a door and throw in a bucket of beetroot and a few pieces of bread. Sometimes they stopped for hours, and a guard would shout for them to hand over any valuables they had left.

Anne, Margot, Peter, and Judy sat together, talking quietly and occasionally climbing up on the bars to peep out of a long hole in the wooden slats. A young man who was keeping watch stepped aside for them; he had been trying to figure out whether they really were headed for Poland, as the rumors had said.

At night it was impossible to sleep. The jarring of the cattle trucks, the smell, and the fear kept them all awake. Tempers frayed and people argued, shouted, and sobbed. Everyone was exhausted. In his memoir, Mr. Frank recalled the journey in just two sentences: "The awful transportation—three days locked in a cattle truck—was the last time I saw my family. Each of us tried to be as courageous as possible and not to let our heads drop."

On the night of the third day, the train began to slow down. The passengers got to their feet, steeling themselves. A murmur of prayer filled the cattle cars. The train turned sharply in the direction of a long, low building with an arched entrance and a high, pointed roof. Searchlight beams swept across marshland, and in the distance, dogs barked fiercely.

The train stopped. Rifle butts pounded on the doors and German voices began to shout, "Jews, out, quickly, OUT!"

NINE:

"WHO HAS INFLICTED THIS UPON US?"

About 216,000 Jewish children were sent to Auschwitz. Just under 7,000 were allowed into the camp to work; the rest were sent to the gas chambers. When Auschwitz was liberated in January 1945, only 451 Jews under the age of sixteen were alive.

In theory, children under the age of fifteen did not exist in Auschwitz. Because they were too weak to withstand the punishing work in the camp, they were usually sent to the gas chambers as soon as they arrived, along with their mothers. A few children survived the selection on the ramp, when newcomers were separated into two groups: those who would live and those who would die. Some of the children who were allowed into Auschwitz were used as guinea pigs in scientific experiments, and others were judged strong enough to work. The only children certain to survive the first selection for the gas chambers were twins. Josef Mengele, the SS doctor in charge of the selections, was fascinated by twins and eager to use them in his experiments. Some were no more than five years old. But Mengele's experiments were so cruel that hardly any of the 3,000 twins admitted to Auschwitz survived.

On September 5, 1944, when the doors of the Westerbork train were wrenched apart, the first thing Anne Frank and her family saw were the glaring searchlights fixed on the train, and outside on the platform, men running back and forth. The men were Kapos (head prisoners), and they reached into the carriages to pull those nearest to them down to the uneven ground. Behind the Kapos, SS officers greeted the Nazi guards who had accompanied the train from Holland.

The Kapos yelled at the newcomers to hurry. There were shouts and screams of anguish as relatives disappeared from view. The Kapos rushed through, dragging luggage from the train and stacking it at the rear of the platform. The bodies of those who had died during the journey were left beside the suitcases. Above the hissing steam of the cooling train, instructions were bellowed from a loudspeaker: "Women to the left! Men to the right!" Anne watched her father, Hermann van Pels, Peter van Pels, and Fritz Pfeffer being herded away by the SS along with all the other male passengers. It was the last time Anne ever saw her beloved father.

The guards stepped forward, shoving the women into columns of five and then again into two rows. The selection to decide who would live and who would die began. Anne stood with her mother and Margot and Mrs. van Pels on the platform, watching as Mengele moved among the crowd. His silver hair gleamed in the light. With a flick of his wrist, he sent Anne, Mrs. Frank, Margot, and Mrs. van Pels to join the line of those who would live.

The loudspeaker roared again: "It's an hour's march to the women's camp. For children and the sick we've provided trucks at the end of the platform. Hurry!" The trucks were painted with red crosses and people ran toward them, hanging on desperately as the motors started up. Within minutes, the people on the trucks had disappeared. None of them were ever seen again.

Anne's group was forced to march quickly. They saw the blue gleam of the electrified fences that ran the length of the camp and silhouetted figures standing motionless in the watchtowers. This was Birkenau, the women's camp in Auschwitz, the greatest death factory of all. There was no longer any doubt about where they were.

The women were led into a narrow building and forced to undress. They stood under the showers while their clothes were taken away. They were then shaved of all their hair. Finally they were given the camp uniform: shoes and a gray sacklike dress, some with crosses on the back marking them out as new arrivals. Wearing their sacks, they went across to a row of desks where they gave their personal details and had their forearms tattooed with their prisoner number. All newcomers were then assigned to their barracks. Anne, Margot, Mrs. Frank, Mrs. de Winter, and her daughter Judy were all placed in Block 29 (Mrs. van Pels had become separated from them in the panic). It was a block identical to all the others: a long, low room in semipermanent darkness, with rows of wooden bunks in tiers of three filled with straw or straw mattresses. The floor swam with urine and excrement.

Each day of Anne's existence in Auschwitz followed the same punishing routine of rising at three thirty A.M., then rushing to the latrine block and back for "breakfast." Every woman had to hang on to the bowl she had been given for her food; the bowls could not be replaced if they were lost, except through "organizing"—camp slang for stealing or bartering. Anne got a pair of men's long underwear from another woman by "organizing" them. Mrs. de Winter recalled: "We had no clothing apart from a gray sack, and under that we were naked. But when the weather turned cold, Anne came into the barracks one day wearing a suit of men's long underwear. She looked screamingly funny with those long white legs, but somehow still charming."

After breakfast came roll call. Anne and the other women had to stand in rows of five in the square while block leaders counted them. Roll call in the morning usually lasted forty-five minutes. Evening roll call could last from an hour to five hours. The women were forced to stand in sun, rain, hail, and snow for as long as the roll call leader chose and while punishments were carried out. Ronnie Goldstein–van Cleef, who had been in Westerbork with the Franks, often stood beside Anne during roll call. They always shared a mug of "coffee," although the liquid didn't taste much like real coffee. Margot stood nearby, either next to Anne or in front of her, depending on how the rows of five worked out.

The march to work took half an hour from Anne's block. The work itself consisted of digging an area of grass and tossing the dirt in a pile. It was completely pointless, but the Kapos ran among them constantly, screaming, "Faster! Faster!" and beating those who couldn't work quickly enough. At twelve thirty P.M., huge vats of soup were carried into the field. Each woman held out her bowl and received one ladle's worth of greasy fluid. For half an hour, they sat in groups of five, drinking from their bowls, and then returned to work. At six o'clock they were given their evening meal: a slice of bread and a tiny piece of margarine. The block leader's assistant distributed the bread. Anne was made an assistant. Mrs. de Winter remembered: "Anne was the youngest in her group, but nevertheless she was the leader of it. She also distributed the bread in the barracks, and she did it so well and so fairly that there was none of the usual grumbling." At nine P.M., the whistles blew and they were allowed into the barracks.

Although the prisoners had survived the selection on the platform when they arrived, they were under constant threat of being sent to the gas chambers. There were regular selections in all the barracks, and no one knew when it might be their turn. Four gas chambers in the camp worked day and night, and during the time of Anne's imprisonment in Auschwitz, as many as 24,000 people were gassed in a single day. Unsurprisingly, the prisoners needed one another for support, and they tried to remain in groups of family and friends as long as possible. Anne, her mother and sister, and Mrs. de Winter and her daughter Judy stayed with three women they had known in Westerbork: Bloem Evers–Emden, Lenie de Jong–van Naarden, and Ronnie Goldstein–van Cleef. Bloem recalls that Mrs. Frank and her two daughters were always together and gave one another a great deal of support. Mrs. Frank's only thought was for her daughters. She stayed with them constantly and tried her hardest to find them something to eat.

On October 27, there was a selection in Anne's block. This time it wasn't for the gas chambers but for work in a Czechoslovakian munitions factory, making weapons for the Nazi war effort. Everyone desperately wanted to be chosen, knowing that they would have a far greater chance of survival outside Auschwitz. Judy de Winter and Bloem Evers–Emden were among those taken. Anne, Margot, and their mother remained in Auschwitz. They were rejected because Anne had scabies, a disease caused by lice getting under the skin and creating painful red and black sores that itch intensely. Mrs. Frank and Margot wouldn't leave Anne alone in the camp, even though it put their own lives at risk. Bloem spoke to Mrs. Frank, who was with Margot. Anne was in the scabies barracks. Mrs. Frank said, "We are, of course, staying with her." Margot nodded. Bloem understood how they felt, and that they were unable to abandon Anne for their own sakes. It was the last time she saw them.

Soon after Anne was put in the scabies barracks, Margot joined her there voluntarily. Lenie de Jong–van Naarden remembers that Mrs. Frank was in complete despair about her daughters. She refused to eat the tiny piece of bread she was given as her rations each day. Instead, she asked Lenie to dig a hole beneath the wooden wall of the scabies barracks, where the ground was quite soft. Mrs. Frank stood beside her the whole time, asking, "Is it working?" Lenie told her that it was. When the hole was big enough, they were able to speak to Margot and Anne, and pass the bread through to them. Inevitably, Margot also caught scabies. Ronnie Goldstein–van Cleef, who was in the barracks with them and another girl named Frieda Brommet, remembered how Frieda's mother and Mrs. Frank searched the entire camp looking for scraps of food to give to the sick girls.

On one occasion, Ronnie found a platinum watch inside her mattress where a previous prisoner had hidden it. She slipped it through the hole underneath the barracks to Mrs. Frank and Mrs. Brommet, who exchanged it for a whole loaf of bread, a piece of cheese, and a piece of sausage. Margot and Anne needed all the food they could get, because their health was failing rapidly. Ronnie remembers that the two girls hardly spoke to anyone. They livened up slightly when the food arrived, but only to share it and eat. Ronnie sometimes sang for them, trying to keep up their spirits. She was shocked by their appearance: They looked terrible, covered in spots and sores from the scabies. They put some ointment on their wounds, but it didn't help.

On October 30, 1944, there was another selection in the women's camp at Auschwitz-Birkenau. Only sixty miles away, the Russians were advancing. The cry of "Block closed!" went up at evening roll call. Anne and Margot and their mother, together with the friends they had made in Westerbork, were among those marched to the large square and forced to undress. They remained there, naked, for two days. Their friend Lientje Brilleslijper recalled: "We stood there. Standing, standing, then a few steps and then standing again, with only a small piece of hard bread for nourishment. Then we were whipped into a big hall where it was at least warm. Here the selection took place."

Josef Mengele stood impatiently beside the blue gleam of the spotlights. Lientje recalled: "He made us step on a scale and then waved his hand right or left to indicate life or death. Just a casual wave—to the gas chamber." Mrs. de Winter was with Mrs. Frank, Margot, and Anne in the line. "It took a long time," she remembered. "We saw that he picked out a great many who were not too old or sick and then we knew that they would escape and that the old and the sick would be gassed." To save themselves, the women took several years off their actual age and lied about their health. Mrs. de Winter called out, "I am twenty-nine and I have never had dysentery yet." But Mengele sent her to join the old and the sick—those who would be gassed. Then it was Mrs. Frank's turn, and he sent her, too, to join the same group.

"Next!" Mengele shouted.

Anne and Margot walked forward. They were still in pitiful condition from the scabies, but they were both young. Mrs. de Winter and Mrs. Frank waited in terror, hoping desperately that they would not join their group on the right. The women on the left did not know what their fate would be, but at least they would not be sent to the gas chambers.

Mrs. de Winter remembered watching the two girls: "Fifteen and eighteen years old, thin, naked but proud, approaching the selection table with the SS men . . . Anne encouraged Margot, and Margot walked erect into the light. There they stood for a moment, naked and shaven-headed, and Anne looked over at us with her unclouded face, looked straight and stood straight. . . ."

"To the left!" Mengele shouted, and Anne and Margot walked on.

Jewish women and children undergoing selections at Auschwitz.
Dr. Josef Mengele sent many immediately to the gas chamber.

At that moment of separation from her daughters, Mrs. Frank let out an anguished scream: "The children! O God, the children . . . !"

Mrs. Frank never saw her daughters again. Although she and Mrs. de Winter were rescued from the gas chambers by a prisoner who managed to drag them away from the waiting line, Mrs. Frank never recovered from losing her children. Without them, and separated from her husband, she lost the will to live.

Edith Frank died of hunger and distress in Auschwitz on January 6, 1945.

Gradually the war was coming to an end. Germany was losing ground on all fronts, and German cities were heavily bombed by the Allies, killing thousands. In Auschwitz, the SS began to destroy all evidence of their crimes. Gassings stopped in November of 1944, and the gas chambers were destroyed. The cremating pits, containing mounds of human ash, were raked over and planted with grass seed. Some of the Kanada warehouses—which contained the clothes and possessions of prisoners—were set on fire, and thousands of documents were burned. In mid-January of 1945, the SS abandoned Auschwitz. The Russians were closing in, and the fleeing SS decided to evacuate all prisoners able to walk.

Across Europe, survivors of ghettos, deportations, slave

labor, and concentration camps were herded through the countryside on "death marches" away from the liberators. Most had to walk in freezing temperatures; others were put on open trucks. Prisoners, starved and beaten by the German guards accompanying them, were sometimes mistaken for German military by Russian soldiers, who would open fire on them. Most of the prisoners died of exhaustion; those who couldn't keep up were shot and their bodies left where they had died.

The death marches were a cheap way of getting prisoners away from the Allied liberators and into the concentration camps of Germany, where they were put to work or left to die without food, water, or medical attention. For many of the prisoners, their destination was Bergen-Belsen. The camp, in northern Germany, had been set up as a prisoner-of-war camp for French and Belgian soldiers, but since 1943, Jews had been sent there and the camp had been taken over by the SS. They began bringing in sick prisoners from other camps, although there was no medication, sanitation, or care for them and almost no food. In December a new commandant, Josef Kramer, arrived from Auschwitz with his cruelest staff. He put Kapos in charge of the camp and starved prisoners deliberately.

By early 1945, the camp was swollen with death-march survivors. There was even less food and water than before, and desperate prisoners ate grass to fill their empty stomachs. Then a typhus epidemic broke out.

Anne and Margot left Auschwitz in a transport of 634 women at the beginning of November 1944, after the selection. They had been given old clothing, odd shoes, a blanket, a quarter of a loaf of bread, five ounces of sausage, and a piece of margarine for their journey. No one knew where they were going, but the journey in the cattle cars was appalling. It was bitterly cold and cramped in the wagons, and they received no more food or water. After four days, the train stopped, and the SS guards unbolted the doors. The exhausted, frozen women climbed out onto the platform at Celle Station. A few miles away was the concentration camp of Bergen-Belsen.

Lientje and Janny Brilleslijper were also on the transport from Auschwitz. As they wandered about Belsen, they met Margot and Anne again. Lientje recalled: "We had a look around, and heard that there was a tap on a little hill. We hurried there to wash. And as the two of us went up the hill, two thin figures approached, and we fell about one another's necks. The two spoke Dutch. We were four shaven-headed figures, thin and shaking. Anne and Margot had many questions, and we, too, had many questions. We asked about their mother, for we knew that in Auschwitz the men had been separated from the group. Anne began to cry bitterly, and Margot said quite softly, 'Selected.'"

The four girls sat together on the hill, watching the

line of exhausted prisoners from Celle Station approach. Lientje looked at Anne and Margot as they huddled beneath their blankets: "The two were inseparable, like my sister and I. They looked like two frozen birds, it was painful to look at them. After we had washed, naked in the open air, we were speedily dressed, for we had nothing except a dress and a thin blanket, a blanket which one treasured like a costly possession. Then we crept together in one of the tents."

Anne and Margot argued at first over whether to enter the tents, but decided it would be better than staying outside. Janny Brilleslijper recalled that they waited until the last moment and then went into the tent. It was boiling hot inside from the number of people herded in there together. It stank terribly, and the rain lashed down on the roof, breaking holes in the tent. They slept on thin layers of straw, cramped together with two hundred others. There was no lighting and no toilets.

On the evening of November 7, a wild storm broke out over the field. The gale ripped up the tents and threw them to the ground. Women screamed and cowered as tent poles crashed down around them. They crouched in the open air, in the pouring rain, until a group of SS guards arrived and drove them into the kitchen tent, hitting them as they ran. The following day, still shivering with the cold, they were moved on again. "We were put in an old barn filled with rags and old shoes," Lientje remembered. "Anne asked, 'Why do they want us to become animals?'"

For a few days, the Brilleslijper sisters became separated from Margot and Anne. Eventually, they ended up in the same barrack, sleeping on wooden bunks in a stone hut, where several thousand people had only one bathroom among them. Before long, the camp was like a huge open sewer, and those who had died were left where they were. More transports kept arriving from other camps, and Belsen became dangerously overcrowded.

Anne and Margot had the bunk below Lientje and Janny in their barrack. Their spirits had not yet been completely broken by the misery surrounding them. "Anne used to tell stories after we lay down," Lientje remembered. "So did Margot. Silly stories and jokes. We all took turns telling them. Mostly they were about food. Once we talked about going to the American Hotel in Amsterdam for dinner and Anne suddenly burst into tears at the thought that we would never get back." The girls were put to work in the shoe shed, a former horse stable where old shoes from Germany lay in huge piles. The shoes had to be unstitched by hand, the leather soles ripped away, and the usable pieces put to one side. The work was difficult and painful, made worse by the constant beatings they received from the SS. Lientje and Anne found it impossible, as Lientje recalled: "Our hands began to fester. Several people died of blood poisoning. Anne and I were the first who had to stop working. Margot and my sister stood it for rather longer, but they shared their food with us . . . we got for this a little more watery soup and a piece of bread. . . . Anne and I began to 'organize' things, to steal from the kitchen or to beg . . . but we never stole from another prisoner. We only stole from the Nazis."

At the end of November, Mrs. van Pels arrived in the camp. Margot and Anne had not seen her since the journey from Westerbork two months before. She immediately became part of their small group. She was with them when they celebrated Christmas and Hanukkah in the camp, having gathered all the scraps of food they could find. Crouched under the sloping roof of their barrack, the women sang their favorite "Jewish songs," Lientje remembered, "and wept. Anne's eyes glittered. She told us stories. We thought they must be old stories which we did not happen to know. But now I know that they were stories she had made up herself. Margot started to tell a story too, but she could not go on and Anne completed it for her. She said that her father knew much better stories and Margot began to cry, asking whether he was still alive. Anne was confident, 'Of course he is alive.'"

Whenever a new transport arrived in the camp, Anne always wanted to know whether any of her friends from Amsterdam were on it. Lientje remembered: "We were taken to another part of the camp. A group of older women and children were also brought there. Anne came excitedly to us, 'Let's go there, maybe there are friends among them, they are said to be all Dutch.' She wanted to go over immediately. At this moment, I believe, she was the Anne whom we know from the diary, mercurial and full of life; at other times I only saw her serious and sad. There were some boys and girls whom Anne knew. . . . She asked after other friends and learned that Lies, a good friend of hers, was quite near, and she could speak to her in the evening if she was careful."

After hearing that Lies was in the camp, Anne rushed to the barbed-wire fence where her friend was waiting. The two girls cried when they saw each other. Lies explained that her mother had died and her father was seriously ill. She was in the camp with her little sister, whom Anne used to babysit in Amsterdam. In contrast to what she had said at Christmas, Anne now told Lies that she believed her father had been killed in Auschwitz. When Anne said that she had nothing to eat, Lies—who still received Red Cross parcels in her part of the camp—brought her food. After one other meeting, the two of them lost contact. Lies's father died, and Lies herself became sick.

In another barrack nearby was a group of Dutch children whom Anne, Margot, Lientje, and Janny visited regularly. They sang to them and told them stories to keep their spirits up. Janny and Lientje also became nurses in a new barrack filled with dying Dutch women and children. They asked Margot and Anne whether they would like to help, but neither girl was strong enough to care for anyone else. The Brilleslijpers stole from the Nazi pharmacy and handed out the medicine to those who needed it most. They lost touch with Anne and Margot, who were moved to another barrack. Lientje eventually found out where they were and went to visit them. "Margot had an attack of dysentery and could not stand and because of the danger of typhus infection she had to stay in the old block," Lientje remembered. "Anne looked after her as well as she could. We were able to bring them a little food which we had organized. A few days later we heard that they were in the sick bay. We went there and urged them not to stay because if they stayed lying they would perish. But it was at least warm there and there were only two of them in the bunk. Anne said, 'We are together and we have our peace.' Margot scarcely said anything. She had a high fever and smiled contentedly. Her mind was already wandering. . . ."

Although it was obvious that a German surrender would soon be declared, the Nazis still went on with their Final Solution until the very end. On April 20, 1945, one of the last groups of Jewish children alive in Germany was killed in Hamburg.

The children—ten boys and ten girls—had been sent from Auschwitz to the Neuengamme concentration camp for use in medical experiments in November of 1944.

They were aged between five and twelve years old and had come from all over Europe. On April 20, SS doctor Kurt Heissmeyer and his assistant, Arnold Strippel, decided to kill the children so that the Allied liberators would not find out about their experiments. Heissmeyer sent the children to the old Bullenhuser Damm school in Hamburg; it had been used during the war as a sub-camp. The children were killed in the basement there.

After the war, Heissmeyer returned to his old town of Magdeburg and continued to work as a doctor. Eventually his past caught up with him, and in 1966 he was sentenced to life imprisonment. His assistant, Arnold Strippel, was never brought to trial, despite repeated efforts by the parents of the murdered children. He lived the rest of his life unharmed, in a villa in a Frankfurt suburb.

Today the room at Bullenhuser Damm where the children died is kept as a memorial to them. Outside is a beautiful garden where anyone who wants to remember the children can plant a rose in their memory.

In one of Belsen's rotting, overcrowded barracks, Margot and Anne lay in agony with typhus. Their bunk was in one of the worst places of all: beside the barrack door, where drafts came stinging through night and day. Rachel van Amerongen–Frankfoorder, who had not seen either of them since Westerbork, was shocked at the change in them both; they were no longer recognizable, thinner than ever, bald, and with sunken faces. They were very weak, but still went each day to visit the prisoners who received food from the Red Cross, hoping for something to eat. Sometimes they quarreled because of their illness, and whenever anyone came in or went out of the barrack, they screamed, "Close the door! Close the door!" Each day their voices became weaker.

Typhus, caused by infected lice, spread swiftly in Belsen because there were no medicines to fight it. Those ill with the disease, like Margot and Anne, suffered skin rashes, fever, acute headaches, and pain everywhere. When Lientje and her sister visited Margot and Anne again, they knew they did not have long to live: "Margot had fallen from the bunk and was half-unconscious. Anne was already very feverish. She was very friendly and loving, 'Margot will sleep well and when she sleeps I don't need to get up anymore.'"

Margot was too weak to survive the fall onto the cold stone floor. The shock killed her. With her sister dead, Anne now gave up hope, and the typhus took hold of her small, wasted body. Janny remembered that Anne was very sick but stayed on her feet until Margot died. She approached Janny one day wearing only a blanket, nothing else. "I can't stand the fleas and the lice in my clothes," she told Janny. "I've thrown everything away. This is all I have." Janny gave her some clothing and bread. But she saw that Anne had given in to her illness. The death of Margot was more than

Anne could bear. She thought that she had nothing left to live for. Her father had actually been liberated in Auschwitz and was on his way back to Amsterdam, asking everyone he met whether they had news of his daughters, but Anne did not know that.

Just a few days after the death of her sister Margot, Anne died in Belsen, alone.

When Lientje and Janny visited the barrack again, the bunk on which Anne and Margot had lain was empty. They knew immediately that the two girls were dead and searched the pile of corpses until they found them. Lientje remembers: "Four of us laid the thin bodies on a blanket and carried them to the great open grave. We could do no more."

On April 15, 1945, only three weeks after the death of Anne Frank, British troops liberated Belsen.

TEN:

"I WANT TO GO ON LIVING
EVEN AFTER MY DEATH . . ."

On April 30, 1945, Adolf Hitler committed suicide. It was the end of the Nazi reign of terror, the end of the Third Reich. Without their leader to guide them, the German army surrendered on May 7, 1945, and the last concentration camps were liberated.

The reaction of Allied soldiers liberating the concentration camps was one of horror and disbelief. In Bergen-Belsen, British troops made the SS bury some of the 10,000 corpses lying about the camp, but to stop typhus from spreading further, huge pits were dug and the bodies dropped in by bulldozers. People who lived nearby, but said they had known nothing about the camp, were brought in and marched around the barracks. A British army captain told them: "What you will see here is such a disgrace to the German people that their name must be eradicated from the list of civilized nations."

May 3, 1945: young prisoners at Dachau concentration camp
cheer the American troops who liberated them.

Many children, especially those in the camps, could not believe they were free. Eva Geiringer, who had been imprisoned in Auschwitz with her mother, remembers that on January 27, 1945, "We heard someone screaming outside. The barrack door was flung open and a woman yelled, 'There's a bear at the gate! A bear at the gate! Come quickly!' Cautiously, we went outside toward the open gate and there, at the entrance, was the 'bear'—a huge being, covered from head to foot in bearskin with a look of utter amazement on his face. We stood and stared at each other and then carefully, I edged toward him with joy on my face. Our liberator stood at the entrance to the camp, alone and strong. With outstretched arms I ran to him and hugged against him . . . and although our languages were not the same, what I said to him and what he said to me was understood by us both."

Other children had unhappier experiences. A young girl called Cornelia had survived in hiding but knew that her family had been deported to Sobibor. She didn't feel any joy when she was able to leave her hiding place: "The war was over—my reaction on that day: why were they [the public] singing and dancing in the street? The war was over, but I had lost my entire family. I was devastated."

Five-year-old Robert Krell, also in hiding, didn't want to go back to his parents, who had survived, too. He hadn't seen them in three years and couldn't believe that the strangers standing before him were his mother and father: "I cried in protest, and they had to prove I was theirs with photos taken when I was aged about one and a half. Of course, I was actually the luckiest of all children in having my parents alive. Try telling that to a five-year-old with no memory of them, after nearly three years with another family."

New experiences made others realize that their freedom was not a dream but reality. Arek Hersh from Poland was a prisoner on a crowded train headed toward Theresienstadt when he was liberated: "We came to a railway station in a place called Roudnice. . . . After about ten minutes we were ordered to get off the train. I saw a Czech policeman giving boys some bread and meat. One of the Ukrainian SS guards also saw this and he turned his rifle round to get hold of the barrel to hit one of the starving boys over the head. The Czech policeman drew his revolver. He pointed it at the SS guard and said, 'If you touch this child, I will shoot you.' I saw the SS guard immediately put his rifle down and walk away. We realized that something we had never seen before was happening: an SS guard had taken orders from someone else."

For some, facing the world again was a frightening experience. Sixteen-year-old Benjamin Bender was liberated at Buchenwald on April 11, 1945: "I stood up, feeling weak. I stared at the beds around me. Motionless people, wax masks, totally unaware that finally they were free. I wanted to scream, to share with them the moment of joy, but I couldn't. There was no joy in my heart but an aching emptiness. I was afraid to walk out to face the new alien world."

A few children immediately felt that they now had a mission in life, having survived against all the odds. Yehuda Bakon, a death-march survivor, asked an Allied soldier for a pencil and began feverishly drawing all he could remember: the gas chambers, the undressing rooms, and the crematorium, the things he had seen and heard. He had always intended to record everything. "I asked the Sonderkommando men [prisoners who had to work at the gas chambers] to tell me so that if one day I will come out, I will tell the world."

Of the eight people who had hidden in the secret annex, Anne's father, Otto Frank, was the only one who survived. He was still in Auschwitz when it was liberated, living in the hospital there after a severe beating from one of the Kapos. The Russian soldiers who set all the surviving prisoners free handed out clothing and food and separated those who were dying from those who might live. Mr. Frank was given a bunk of his own in a different barrack. He immediately began asking people if they knew what had happened to his wife and daughters. He found out that his wife was dead. From that moment on, Mr.

Frank put all his efforts and hope into the belief that his daughters were still alive. Throughout his long journey by train and boat back to Amsterdam, he asked everyone whom he saw about Margot and Anne, but no one had any news.

Mr. Frank arrived in Amsterdam on June 3, 1945. He went straight to Miep and Jan's apartment. His friends were overwhelmed to see him and told him that he could stay with them as long as he wished. He explained that his wife was dead but that he was sure Margot and Anne were still alive. Miep and Jan were also convinced that the two girls would return. Miep was so certain of this that she did not tell Mr. Frank about the object she kept in her desk at work: Anne's diary.

She had found it on the day of the arrest. After the Gestapo had left the building, she, Jan, and Bep had gone up to the annex. Everything was a complete mess, with drawers pulled open and objects scattered around. The floor was lost under heaps of books and papers. Looking more closely, Miep realized that many of the papers belonged to Anne. She pointed out the diary to Bep, who picked it up. Quickly, the two women sorted through the jumble for anything bearing Anne's handwriting. They also saved a photograph album, schoolbooks, reading books, Anne's shoe bag embroidered with her initials, Anne's combing shawl, and a little book of quotations compiled by Anne. Returning to the office, Miep placed the diary in her desk, determined to keep it under lock and key until she could hand it back to Anne. The diary was Anne's private property, Miep felt, and for this reason she said nothing to Mr. Frank about it.

Immediately after his arrival in Amsterdam, Mr. Frank went back to his old job at the Prinsengracht office. He was delighted to find Kugler and Kleiman there as well. Both had survived imprisonment in Dutch camps. While they had been in prison, Miep had taken charge of the business, but now everybody returned to their old jobs.

When Mr. Frank wasn't working, he spent every spare minute questioning people, checking survivor lists, calling the Red Cross organization, and placing advertisements in the press, all in the hope of finding his daughters. In July he was visiting the Red Cross again when he saw a list with Xs placed beside the names of those known to have died. Margot and Anne were listed—with crosses next to their names. The woman who had informed the Red Cross that the girls were dead was Janny Brilleslijper, who, together with her sister Lientje, had been among the last to see Anne and Margot in Belsen. Mr. Frank visited first Lientje and then Janny at their own homes shortly afterward. Janny told him helplessly, "Your daughters are . . . no more." She watched in horror as he went white and fell into a chair, his last shred of hope gone.

When Miep heard the news, her first thoughts apart from those of deep sorrow were of Anne's diary. She knew she now had to give it to Mr. Frank. At the time, he was sitting alone in his office with his head in his hands. She placed the small pile of papers and books on his desk and said softly, "Here is your daughter Anne's legacy to you." On top lay the red-and-white-checked diary. Miep left the room and Mr. Frank opened the book in a daze. Its pages were untouched since Anne herself had last written in it. And there she was, on the first page, smiling up at him from a school photograph.

Slowly, Mr Frank began to read: "Gorgeous photograph isn't it!!! . . . On Friday, 12th June, I woke up at six o'clock and no wonder; it was my birthday. . . ."

Although some survivors of the concentration camps made their way back home by ship and train, many remained in the displaced-persons' camps set up by the Allies. In December of 1946, there were approximately 160,000 Jews living in West German displaced-persons' camps, the largest of which was in the old army camp in Bergen-Belsen. They were cared for by the British army and a number of international charities who gave them food and other necessities.

There were many orphaned children in the displaced-persons' camps who needed special care after their experiences. Older children were given courses in different languages and took part in training programs. Through the Youth Aliyah (Youth Immigration) organization, thousands of child survivors moved to Palestine, which became the Jewish state of Israel in 1948. Many felt that they could no longer live in the countries where they had been persecuted and lost their families, and where anti-Semitism still existed. The creation of a safe Jewish homeland was very important to them for this reason.

Few of those children who had been sent to Britain in 1938 and 1939 on the Kindertransports were reunited with their families, almost all of whom had perished in the camps. Those who did find their parents again usually met one another as strangers. One young woman arranged for her mother to join her in England, but it was not as she had expected: "It was a very strange experience. I was a little girl when I left and now I was a woman with a baby. Although it was August [my mother] was wearing a fur coat to bring it with her. She was a stranger to me; it was terrible. It didn't get any easier; it was always difficult."

Approximately half the Jewish children who had hidden in Holland with foster families during the war were reunited with their parents. Others stayed with their host families, and some children were never told the truth about their backgrounds. Jewish children who had survived the camps were usually placed with foster families. Among them was Bronia Davidson, who described her return to school: "In class Death had taken its seat next to every child. A few children had two parents, like Anna, a spirited girl, who not only had parents, but a little brother as well. My friend Sara lived with a stepmotherly aunt. All replacement mothers were evil stepmothers, who couldn't match the beautiful memory of the mother we sometimes had hardly known. How faithful we were to those buried, gassed, executed parents."

Eva Geiringer, returning to Holland with her mother, found it very strange to move back into their former apartment. She recalls: "It felt so eerie to walk up the stairs. Inside it was as if the intervening years had not taken place. It was like stepping back in time—everything looked exactly the same. I wandered in and out of the rooms. Our furniture was in the same place, the curtains and the paintwork was unchanged and when I looked for the spot on my bedroom wall where Pappy [her father] had marked my height, it was still there. I went to the window and looked down into the square. Some children were playing at one end on the tarmac. Later I heard a taxi draw up in the street below and ran to open the door thinking, *That's Pappy coming home with Heinz.* But it was only a neighbour from across the hall." Eva's father and brother did not come back; both had died in Mauthausen. Eva moved to London in the 1950s, where she married and had three children.

In late summer of 1945, the first photographs of the concentration camps were published in newspapers throughout the world, shocking everyone. A year later, twenty-two leaders of the Nazi party were put on trial

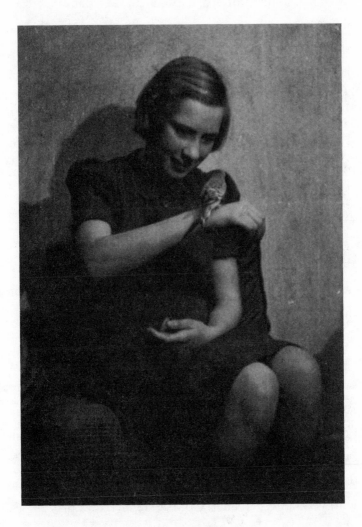

Eva Geiringer Schloss

before the Nuremberg Tribunal in Germany. Of those, only twelve were sentenced to hang. Among their number was Martin Bormann, who died before the execution date, and Hermann Goring, who killed himself rather than face the hangman's rope. Ten former Nazis were hanged on October 16, 1946, but many of those who had committed the most terrible crimes escaped justice, some by fleeing to Britain, the United States, Canada, and Argentina, where they lived the rest of their lives without ever having to account for what they had done. One was Josef Mengele, Auschwitz's "Angel of Death" who had been in charge of the selections and performed medical experiments on hundreds of children. He escaped to Latin America and died in a swimming accident in Brazil in 1979.

In other countries, too, followers of the Nazi movement were put on trial. A few were hanged; most served only a few years in prison before being allowed to go free. About 10,000 high-ranking Nazis managed to escape before the courts caught up with them. Some were found by a concentration-camp survivor, Simon Wiesenthal, who dedicated his life to hunting them down. Adolf Eichmann, who was largely in charge of the deportation process, was discovered living in Argentina by Israeli forces that kidnapped him, then brought him to trial in Israel. He was executed in 1962.

With the knowledge that both his children were dead, Mr. Frank turned his efforts to finding people he had known before the war. He already knew that his friends who had hidden with him had died in different camps: Mr. van Pels had been gassed in Auschwitz; Fritz Pfeffer had been transferred to Neuengamme concentration camp, where he died on December 20, 1944; Peter van Pels had been taken to Mauthausen on a death march and died on May 5, 1945; and Mrs. van Pels died in an unknown location sometime before May 8, 1945. However, Anne's friends Lies Goslar and Jacqueline van Maarsen were still alive, and Mr. Frank visited them often. He also wrote to his family in Switzerland, and in one letter he mentioned Anne's diary for the first time: "I don't have any photos from the last years of course, but Miep by chance saved an album and Anne's diary. But I didn't have the strength to read it all."

Soon, though, Mr. Frank did begin to read the diary and found it difficult to put down. In his memoir, written many years later, he explained how he had felt at that time: "I began to read slowly, only a few pages each day, more would have been impossible, as I was overwhelmed by painful memories. For me, it was a revelation. There, was revealed a completely different Anne to the child that I had lost. I had no idea of the depth of her thoughts and feelings . . . through Anne's accurate description of every event and every person, all the details of being in hiding become clear to me again."

Mr. Frank copied out the diary for his mother and sister in Switzerland, using a combination of Anne's original diary and the version she rewrote with a view to publication. He left out the parts he thought were less interesting and those entries where Anne had written most angrily about her mother. He asked a friend to help him translate Anne's words from Dutch into German, because his mother knew no Dutch. Mr. Frank mailed the whole thing bit by bit to his mother. His family there was astonished by it, as was his friend, Werner Cahn, who told him he thought it should be published. Mr. Frank thought about it and in the end decided that it was what Anne would have wanted. In his memoir he wrote, "Anne would have so much loved to see something published. . . . Initially I was very reluctant to publish, but then again and again I saw that my friends were right . . . the first edition of the diary appeared in 1947. Anne would have been so proud."

The first Dutch edition, published in June of 1947 on what would have been Anne's eighteenth birthday, sold out after six months and a second edition was printed to meet the demand. Mr. Frank then sent the manuscript to publishers in Germany, who were undecided about bringing it out at first, feeling it might stir up a lot of emotion and guilt among the German people, but when it appeared in Germany in 1950 it sold well. The diary was published in France and Japan that same year, where it was a success, and appeared in Britain two years later. In America it became an instant best seller.

By the mid-1950s, Mr. Frank was spending several hours a day answering the letters he received from people who had read the diary. So popular had Anne's words become that in 1955, a play based on the diary opened in New York in America. It was highly successful and won many awards, going on tour throughout Europe. More than a million people saw the play in Germany, and sales of the diary soared. Youth groups there were established in Anne's name, schools and streets were named after her, a crowd of 2,000 teenagers traveled to Bergen-Belsen to commemorate her death, and at her former home in Frankfurt, a plaque was attached to the wall. In 1959, a Hollywood film, *The Diary of Anne Frank*, was released.

Ever since the earliest publication of the diary, people had knocked on the door of 263 Prinsengracht, asking if they could look around the secret annex. On May 3, 1960, it officially opened as a museum called the Anne Frank House. Several changes were made to the front house where the offices and warehouse had been, but the annex was kept as near as possible to how it had looked when Anne had been in hiding there. However, Mr. Frank insisted that the annex should remain empty, as it had been left after the arrest when the Nazis took away all their furniture and belongings.

After retiring from his businesses, Mr. Frank moved to

Switzerland. He had recently married again; Fritzi, his second wife, was the mother of Eva Geiringer, and was herself a Holocaust survivor. Fritzi helped her husband with the vast amount of correspondence produced by Anne's diary, which Mr. Frank took with him to Switzerland. For the rest of his life, Mr. Frank had to deal with extremists—people who said that his daughter's diary was a fake, written by someone else after the war to make money. The diary has undergone a series of scientific tests, which have proved, beyond doubt, that it is a real document written by Anne Frank and no one else.

Mr. Frank was in good health until the last year of his life, when he became ill with cancer. He died on August 19, 1980, at home in Switzerland. He was ninety-one years old. His second wife, Fritzi, outlived her husband by eighteen years. She spent the last months of her life living with her daughter in London. Today, Miep Gies is the sole surviving member of the five helpers. They were all given the highest honor possible to those who helped Jews during wartime: They were each awarded the accolade of "the Righteous of the Nations" by Yad Vashem, the Holocaust memorial center in Israel.

One thing has always intrigued readers of the diary over the years: Who told the Nazis about the occupants of the secret annex? There were two official investigations into the matter during Mr. Frank's lifetime, but neither came up with a definitive answer. Until someone finds the receipt for the money the betrayer would have received for making that fateful telephone call (if the receipt still exists), the mystery will endure.

More than 20,000 Jewish communities were destroyed in Europe between 1940 and 1945. This figure, just like all the figures in the Holocaust, is so vast that it is hard to imagine what it actually represents.

Moniek Goldberg, who was a child survivor of the camps, was at first hurt by people's failure to understand: "But as I grew older I came to realize that I could not expect people to understand. . . . The tragedy that befell our people was so great, so complete, that one cannot imagine it." Moniek emigrated from Britain to America and set up a successful business in Florida, where he lives with his family. "When I look at my children and the children of my friends I realize more than ever that the victory is ours. We are able and useful citizens of society, with families who give us a lot to be proud of."

As many former concentration camps became museums, some survivors returned to the places where they had been imprisoned as children. It gave them a feeling of strength, as Erwin Baum, who returned to Auschwitz in June of 1988, explains: "I went to the bunk where I slept. I went to where they put on my number. I went to the bench where they beat us. When I was thirteen and went there for the first time, there was no way out. This time I walked in because I wanted to, and on the other side of the gate there was a taxi waiting for me whenever I wanted to leave. I felt truly liberated for the first time. I had walked in and out of my own free will." To those who say that the Holocaust didn't take place, Erwin has a firm answer: "To the people who say there was no Holocaust, tell them I was there. I'm real. It happened."

The Nazis who faced trial often claimed to have been merely acting on orders. But it *was* possible to resist those orders, which were to persecute and to kill. However evil their actions, the Nazis themselves were human beings and many of them had homes and families that they loved. Nonetheless, they chose to obey their orders. A few did resist, and even rescued Jews. The case of Oskar Schindler is probably the most well known because of the book and then the film *Schindler's List*. He saved 1,200 Jews by giving them employment in his factories in Krakow and Brünnlitz, between 1943 and 1944. At first he seemed no different from any other Nazi; he lived in an apartment that became empty when the Jewish family who owned it was turned out, and his factory had also belonged to a Jewish man. But gradually, his eyes opened to what was happening. He did all he could to protect the Jews who worked for him, even defying Nazi orders to transfer some of his employees to a slave-labor camp, and when three hundred of his female workers were sent to Auschwitz by mistake (during the transferral of his factory from one town to another), he personally visited the camp to get them out. His wife, Emilie, helped to care for many of the workers. When Schindler died in October of 1974, more than four hundred Jews whom he had rescued attended his funeral in Jerusalem, and today there are more than 6,000 descendants of "Schindler Jews" living all over the world.

Many people claimed not to know what was happening to the Jews at the time. Some people simply did not want to know.

"Not to choose is also a choice," wrote French philosopher Albert Camus. In the end, perhaps, it is the most dangerous choice of all. There are still cases of genocide taking place in the world today, but none of it is inevitable. It does not have to happen; it isn't fate. It is up to the individual, to all of us, to make a difference.

Anne's diary is now in Amsterdam once again, on display in the secret annex. It has become a phenomenon, and Anne herself is now a historical figure. There are Anne Frank roses and tulips, statues, stamps, medals, and awards, an Anne Frank Day held annually on June 12, and exhibitions about her throughout the world. A forest of 10,000 trees grows in her honor in Israel, a wax statue of her sits in Amsterdam's Madame Tussaud's, the Anne Frank House receives a million visitors each year, and yet behind all this is a very ordinary girl . . . with an extraordinary gift for writing.

When, in her shuttered room, Anne mused, "Will I ever be able to write anything great?" she had no idea just how powerful her words would become. Her diary is now seen as "the most important source of knowledge in the world today concerning the Holocaust"; "the most widely read book of World War II"; "one of the key writings of the twentieth century"; and is a set text in schools everywhere.

"I want to go on living, even after my death!" she wrote. Her diary has ensured that she will.

ADDITIONAL INFORMATION AND RESOURCES

JEWISH POPULATIONS OF EUROPE BEFORE THE WAR

This table lists the estimated Jewish populations of major European countries before World War II and the Holocaust.

Poland = 3,225,000

Ukraine = 1,500,000

Russia = 975,000

Belorussia = 375,000

Lithuania = 153,743

Latvia = 93,479

Estonia = 4,566

Romania = 796,000

Germany = 554,000

Hungary = 473,000

Czechoslovakia = 356,830

France = 300,000

Great Britain = 300,000

Austria = 181,778

Holland = 170,000

Belgium = 90,000

Greece = 77,000

Yugoslavia = 70,000

Bulgaria = 50,000

Italy = 48,000

Denmark = 5,577

Luxembourg = 5,000

Finland = 2,000

Norway = 1,728

Albania = 200

Total = 9,807,901

JEWISH POPULATIONS OF EUROPE AFTER THE WAR

This table lists the estimated Jewish populations of major European countries after World War II and the Holocaust.

Poland = 325,000

Ukraine = 600,000

Russia = 868,000

Belorussia = 130,000

Lithuania = 13,743

Latvia = 23,479

Estonia = 3,066

Romania = 526,000

Germany = 424,000

Hungary = 23,000

Czechoslovakia = 205,830

France = 210,000

Great Britain = 299,870

Austria = 131,778

Holland = 64,000

Belgium = 65,000

Greece = 12,000

Yugoslavia = 10,000

Bulgaria = 38,600

Italy = 40,500

Denmark = 5,517

Luxembourg = 4,000

Finland = 1,993

Norway = 858

Albania = 200

Total = 4,026,434

SOURCE NOTES

All chapter titles are from *The Diary of Anne Frank*.

ONE: "AS WE ARE JEWISH . . ."

"A real little rich . . ." Frank, *The Diary of Anne Frank: The Critical Edition*, May 8, 1944. All quotations from Anne's diary are taken from this edition.

"None but members . . ." Quoted in Gilbert, *Never Again: A History of the Holocaust*, p. 38.

"Mother and Margot visit . . ." and "Anne does so . . ." Anne Frank's baby book in the archives of the Anne Frank-Fonds, Basel.

"My brother and I . . ." Elias, author interview, October 1997.

"We'll find out soon enough . . ." Schnabel, *The Footsteps of Anne Frank*, p. 24.

"The media were . . ." Quoted in Anne Frank Stichting, *Anne Frank: A History for Today*, p. 20.

"Won't anyone stand up . . ." Schick, *The Story Within Her Story*.

"Well, let's see . . ." Steenmeijer and Frank, *A Tribute to Anne Frank*, p. 13.

TWO: "WE EMIGRATED TO HOLLAND . . ."

"As early as 1932 . . ." Metselaar, van der Rol, Stam, and Gales Loot, *Anne Frank House: A Museum with a Story*, p. 16.

"A youth will grow . . ." Rauschning, *The Voice of Destruction*, p. 252.

"Huge men . . ." Quoted in van Last Galen and Wolfswinkel, *Anne Frank and After: Dutch Holocaust Literature in Perspective*, p. 25.

"When we've settled . . ." Quoted in Anne Frank Stichting, *Anne Frank: A History for Today*, p. 34.

"The Jewish nose . . ." Cited in Shawn, *The End of Innocence: Anne Frank and the Holocaust*, p. 8.

"These are children . . ." Cited in Anne Frank Stichting, *Anne Frank in the World*.

"Our class was given . . ." Quoted in Brown, Stephens, and Rubin, *Images from the Holocaust: A Literature Anthology*, p. 15.

"I screamed . . ." Quoted in Brown, Stephens, and Rubin, *Images of the Holocaust*, p. 24.

"People always said . . ." *The Diary of Anne Frank*, June 15, 1942.

"That's still no reason . . ." Schnabel, *The Footsteps of Anne Frank*, p. 33.

THREE: "WHEN WE WERE STILL IN NORMAL LIFE . . ."

"Anne is not as well . . ." and "Our big girl, Margot . . ." Anne Frank Stichting, *Anne Aus Frankfurt*, exhibition panel.

"Anne wasn't a strong . . ." Otto Frank, memoir, in the private collection of Buddy Elias.

"At the time . . ." and "God knows everything . . ." Quoted in Lindwer, *The Last Seven Months of Anne Frank*, pp. 16–17.

"Dear Omi . . ." Anne Frank, letter, *Stern* magazine, May 21, 1982.

"The Franks were cat . . ." Gies with Gold, *Anne Frank Remembered*, pp. 22–23.

"Boys really liked her . . ." Quoted in Lindwer, *The Last Seven Months of Anne Frank*, pp. 16–17.

"a real problem child . . ." Steenmeijer and Frank, *A Tribute to Anne Frank*, p. 18.

"I had no idea . . ." Elias, author interview, October 1997.

"I adored her because . . ." *You Magazine*.

"With the motto . . ." Hödl, "It Must Never Happen Again," p. 34.

"The Nazis were burning . . ." Quoted in Turner, *And The Policeman Smiled: 10,000 Children Escape from Nazi Europe*, p. 20.

"People would yell . . ." Quoted in Anne Frank Stichting, *Anne Frank: A History for Today*, p. 68.

"Every day the teacher . . ." Quoted in Brown, Stephens, and Rubin, *Images of the Holocaust*, p. 32.

"Our grandmother was living . . ." Elias, author interview, October 1997.

"The atmosphere up and down . . ." Quoted in Turner, *And the Policeman Smiled*, pp. 28–29.

"All I succeeded . . ." Quoted in Turner, *And the Policeman Smiled*, p. 38.

"To serve as a support . . ." Frank, *The Diary of Anne Frank*, September 28, 1942.

"I have often told you . . ." Otto Frank, letter, May 11, 1939, in Frank, *The Diary of Anne Frank*, September 28, 1942.

"Jacque . . ." Frank, *The Diary of Anne Frank*, September 28, 1942.

"Life was hard . . ." Quoted in Gilbert, *Never Again*, p. 47.

"The destruction of . . ." Quoted in Dawidowicz, *The War Against the Jews: 1933–1945*, p. 143.

FOUR: "GOOD TIMES RAPIDLY FLED . . ."

"I saw German soldiers . . ." Quoted in Gilbert, *Never Again*, p. 53.

"During the first months . . ." and "Edith and I discussed . . ." Fussman, "The Woman Who Would Have Saved Anne Frank."

"It is correct . . ." Quoted in Schnabel, *The Footsteps of Anne Frank*, p. 41.

"Anne was a lovely girl. . . ." Quoted in Schnabel, *The Footsteps of Anne Frank*, pp. 42–43.

"She hated maths . . ." Otto Frank, memoir.

"Amsterdam, 29 April, Monday . . ." Letter in the Simon Wiesenthal Center Collection.

"Needless to say . . ." Rubin, *Searching for Anne Frank: Letters from Amsterdam to Iowa.*

"We often talked . . ." Quoted in O'Shaughnessy, "Global Interest Stuns Pen Pals of Anne Frank."

"To be very honest . . ." Quoted in Shepard, "Anne Frank Letter to Iowa Pen Pal to Be Sold."

"We are living our last moments . . ." Quoted in Shawn, *The End of Innocence*, pp. 70–71.

"There are always heaps . . ." Quoted in Schoenberner, *The Yellow Star: The Persecution of the Jews in Europe 1933–1945*, p. 71.

"My little sister complains . . ." and "I go on dreaming . . ." Quoted in Brown, Stephens, and Rubin, *Images from the Holocaust*, p. 171.

"Equal to all . . ." Quoted in Gilbert, *Never Again*, p. 58.

"Things are getting more serious . . ." Frank, *The Diary of Anne Frank*, undated entry.

"This is a photograph of me . . ." Frank, *The Diary of Anne Frank*, October 10, 1942.

FIVE: "WHEN THE SUFFERINGS OF US JEWS REALLY BEGAN . . ."

"The day after the invasion . . ." Frijda, author interview, March 1998.

"During the invasion there were . . ." Schloss, author interview, January 1998.

"Peter crossed my path . . ." *The Diary of Anne Frank*, January 6, 1944.

"Soon we'll have the holidays . . ." Anne Frank, letter, June 1941, in the private collection of Buddy Elias.

"In addition to Anne's . . ." Gies with Gold, *Anne Frank Remembered*, p. 48.

"It was very difficult for Anne . . ." Otto Frank, memoir.

"We lived two stops . . ." Nussbaum, "Life and Death."

"Anne made everything fun . . ." van Maarsen, *A Friend Called Anne*, p. 46.

"Always very sweet . . ." van Maarsen, *My Friend Anne Frank*, pp. 21–22.

"Margot was very clever . . ." van Maarsen, author interview, February 1998.

"Otto was an extrovert . . ." van Maarsen, *My Friend Anne Frank*, p. 46.

"She always had . . ." van Maarsen, *My Friend Anne Frank*, p. 23.

"Dearest mother . . ." Otto Frank, postcard, September 14, 1941, in the private collection of Buddy Elias.

"We're staying here . . ." Anne Frank, postcard, September 14, 1941, in the private collection of Buddy Elias.

"The Fuhrer has given . . ." Quoted in Dawidowicz, *The War Against the Jews*, p. 169.

"Europe will be combed . . ." Quoted in Gilbert, *Never Again*, p. 70.

"Auschwitz would serve . . ." and "Every Jew . . ." Quoted in Lee, *The Hidden Life of Otto Frank*, p. 141.

"They went out . . ." Quoted in Schoenberner, *The Yellow Star*, p. 45.

"No one will ever know . . ." *The Diary of Anne Frank*, June 20, 1942.

"I soon realized . . ." Otto Frank, letter, June 10, 1971, in the private collection of Buddy Elias.

"Jacque used to say . . ." *The Diary of Anne Frank*, June 20, 1942.

"We talked about the laws . . ." van Maarsen, author interview, January 1998.

"Good heavens, if I chewed . . ." Schnabel, *The Footsteps of Anne Frank*, p. 58.

"That one year in the Lyceum . . ." Frank, *Tales from the Secret Annex*, p. 93.

"She was always on the go . . ." Otto Frank, memoir.

"We formed the ping pong . . ." and "We never sat inside . . ." van Maarsen, author interview, January 1998.

"I've been busy . . ." Anne Frank, letter, May 1942, in the private collection of Buddy Elias.

"I said to Mummy . . ." Margot Frank, letter, May 1942, in the private collection of Buddy Elias.

SIX: "IT'S AN ODD IDEA FOR SOMEONE LIKE ME TO KEEP A DIARY . . ."

"All Jews appearing . . ." Quoted in Presser, *Ashes in the Wind: The Destruction of Dutch Jewry*, p. 120.

"I am not going . . ." Quoted in Shawn, *The End of Innocence*, pp. 81–82.

"People always say nowadays . . ." Schloss, author interview, January 1998.

"We were still in bed . . ." Quoted in van Last Galen and Wolfswinkel, *Anne Frank and After*, pp. 47–48.

"Gorgeous photograph . . ." *The Diary of Anne Frank*, June 12, 1942.

"I remember that Anne . . ." Lindwer, *The Last Seven Months of Anne Frank*, p. 31.

"We were very curious . . ." van Maarsen, author interview, January 1998.

"Anne always wrote . . ." van Maarsen, *My Friend Anne Frank*, p. 54.

"With sparkling eyes . . ." van Maarsen, *My Friend Anne Frank*, p. 68.

"If I'd known what . . ." Pick-Goslar and Gold, *Memories of Anne Frank: Reflections of a Childhood Friend*, p. 31.

"She was very attractive . . ." Edmond Silberberg, author interview, June 1998.

"The fulfilment of those . . ." *The Diary of Anne Frank*, July 1, 1942.

"Why of course it does . . ." Schnabel, *The Footsteps of Anne Frank*, p. 36.

"In your own interests . . ." Quoted in Presser, *Ashes in the Wind*, p. 101.

"They closed off the street . . ." and "One of the soldiers . . ." Quoted in Shawn, *The End of Innocence*, p. 75.

"There were screaming children . . ." Quoted in Presser, *Ashes in the Wind*, p. 164.

"We are all well . . ." and "I cannot write . . ." Otto Frank, post-card, July 5, 1942, in the private collection of Buddy Elias.

"We were soaked through . . ." Gies with Gold, *Anne Frank Remembered*, p. 71.

"When we heard . . ." Schnabel, *The Footsteps of Anne Frank*, pp. 60–61.

"Anne's unmade bed . . ." van Maarsen, *My Friend Anne Frank*, pp. 27–28.

SEVEN: "WE HAVE TO WHISPER AND TREAD LIGHTLY . . ."

"Grudgingly, the farmer . . ." Quoted in Gilbert, *Never Again*, p. 102.

"You couldn't imagine . . ." Schloss, author interview, January 1998.

"A very difficult thing . . ." Quoted in Gilbert, *Never Again*, p. 103.

"The priest and his assistant . . ." Quoted in Brown, Stephens, and Rubin, *Images from the Holocaust*, pp. 55–56.

"From the time Mutti . . ." Schloss with Kent, *Eva's Story: A Survivor's Tale by the Step-Sister of Anne Frank*, p. 44.

"They will think . . ." Zapruder, *Salvaged Pages: Young Writers' Diaries of the Holocaust*.

"Had I not religion . . ." Zapruder, *Salvaged Pages*.

"I shall never stop . . ." Zapruder, *Salvaged Pages*.

"Awfully scared . . ." Frank, *The Diary of Anne Frank*, November 28, 1942.

"When someone comes in . . ." Frank, *The Diary of Anne Frank*, December 24, 1943.

"On whose branches . . ." Frank, *The Diary of Anne Frank*, February 23, 1944.

"It won't do us . . ." Frank, *The Diary of Anne Frank*, November 20, 1942.

"I get frightened . . ." Frank, *The Diary of Anne Frank*, November 19, 1942.

"Although I'm only . . ." Frank, *The Diary of Anne Frank*, May 3, 1944.

"It's really a wonder . . ." Frank, *The Diary of Anne Frank*, July 15, 1944.

"Regularly killed . . ." Frank, *The Diary of Anne Frank*, p. 273 footnote.

"One morning on my way . . ." Quoted in Shawn, *The End of Innocence*, p. 83.

"I never felt . . ." Lambert, "A Portrait of Anne Frank."

"No, especially not . . ." *Anne Frank Magazine 1998*, interview with Miep Gies, pp. 26–28.

"It is amazing . . ." *The Diary of Anne Frank*, January 28, 1944.

"Don't worry . . ." Quoted in Shawn, *The End of Innocence*, p. 75.

"It's only a few years . . ." "Long live freedom" and "Their spirit lives . . ." Gill, *Honourable Defeat*, pp. 183–95.

"One—two—three . . ." Reprinted in Brown, Stephens, and Rubin, *Images from the Holocaust*, p. 473.

"I trust to luck . . ." *The Diary of Anne Frank*, February 3, 1944.

"I want to write . . ." *The Diary of Anne Frank*, March 25, 1944.

"Yes . . . no . . . yes . . ." Schnabel, *The Footsteps of Anne Frank*, p. 90.

"if I'm quiet . . ." *The Diary of Anne Frank*, August 1, 1944.

EIGHT: "I AM AFRAID OF PRISON CELLS AND CONCENTRATION CAMPS . . ."

"God? . . ." Klarsfeld, *French Children of the Holocaust: A Memorial*. Reprinted on www.auschwitz.dk/letter.htm.

"Before Brandeis . . ." Newton, "Holocaust Children's Art Collection to Be Shown Outside Prague for First Time."

"Don't move . . . while we've been here." This account and the quotations in it are drawn from interviews with Jan Gies, Miep Gies, and Bep Vokuijl conducted and archived by the Netherlands Institute for War Documentation; Schnabel, *The Footsteps of Anne Frank*; Gies with Gold, *Anne Frank Remembered*; "The Arrest" by Harry Paape in *The Diary of Anne Frank: The Critical Edition*; and Shapiro, *The Reminiscences of Victor Kugler, the 'Mr Kraler' of Anne Frank's Diary*.

"Anne walked back . . ." Pratt, "Anne Frank We Remember," pp. 72–73.

"like beaten dogs" Gies with Gold, *Anne Frank Remembered*, p. 156.

"We hadn't been especially . . ." and "We tried everything . . ." Schloss, author interview, January 1998.

"Mr. Frank was . . ." Cohn, "The Day I Met Anne Frank," pp. 7–8.

"The two girls . . ." Brilleslijper, memoir included in film booklet for *Ein Tagebuch für Anne Frank*.

"Anne was very nice . . ." Lindwer, *The Last Seven Months of Anne Frank*, pp. 92–93.

"Anne's father was quiet . . ." Schnabel, *The Footsteps of Anne Frank*, p. 127.

"At the camp . . ." Otto Frank, memoir.

"By noon inside the wagon . . ." Gryn, *Chasing Shadows: Memories of a Vanished World*.

"On September 2 . . ." Schnabel, *The Footsteps of Anne Frank*, pp. 128–129.

"The awful transportation . . ." Otto Frank, memoir.

NINE: "WHO HAS INFLICTED THIS UPON US?"

"It's an hour's march" Schloss, author interview, January 1998.

"We had no clothing . . ." Quoted in Schnabel, *The Footsteps of Anne Frank*, p. 135.

"Anne was the youngest . . ." Quoted in Schnabel, *The Footsteps of Anne Frank*, p. 135.

"We are, of course . . ." Quoted in Lindwer, *The Last Seven Months of Anne Frank*, p. 129.

"Is it working . . ." Quoted in Lindwer, *The Last Seven Months of Anne Frank*, p. 155.

"We stood there . . ." and "He made us step . . ." Brilleslijper, *Ein Tagebuch für Anne Frank*.

"It took a long time . . ." and "I am twenty-nine . . ." Quoted in Schnabel, *The Footsteps of Anne Frank*, p. 137.

"Fifteen and eighteen . . ." Interview with Rosa de Winter in the archives of the Anne Frank Stichting, Amsterdam.

"Anne encouraged Margot . . ." and "The children! O God . . ." Quoted in Schnabel, *The Footsteps of Anne Frank*, p. 138.

"We had a look around . . . Margot had fallen . . ." This account and the quotations in it are drawn from Brilleslijper, *Ein Tagebuch für Anne Frank*.

"I can't stand the fleas . . ." Quoted in Lindwer, *The Last Seven Months of Anne Frank*, pp. 73–74.

"Four of us laid . . ." Brilleslijper, *Ein Tagebuch für Anne Frank*.

TEN: "I WANT TO GO ON LIVING EVEN AFTER MY DEATH . . ."

"What you will see here . . ." Quoted in Berenbaum, *The World*

Must Know: The History of the Holocaust as Told in the United States Holocaust Memorial Museum, p. 186

"We heard someone . . ." Schloss with Kent, *Eva's Story*, p. 147.

"The war was over . . ." and "I cried in protest . . ." Quoted in van Last Galen and Wolfswinkel, *Anne Frank and After*, p. 121.

"We came to a railway . . ." Quoted in Gilbert, *Never Again*, p. 154.

"I stood up . . ." Quoted in Gilbert, *Never Again*, p. 152.

"I asked the Sonderkommando . . ." Quoted in Gilbert, *The Holocaust: The Jewish Tragedy*, p. 825.

"Your daughters are no more . . ." From an interview with Janny Brilleslijper conducted by Jon Blair for the making of his documentary *Anne Frank Remembered*, Sony Pictures, 1995.

"Here is your daughter Anne's . . ." From an interview with Miep Gies conducted by Jon Blair for the making of his documentary *Anne Frank Remembered*, Sony Pictures, 1995.

"It was a very strange . . ." Quoted in Turner, *And the Policeman Smiled*, p. 272.

"In class Death . . ." Quoted in van Last Galen and Wolfswinkel, *Anne Frank and After*, p. 130.

"It felt so eerie . . ." Schloss with Kent, *Eva's Story*, p. 216.

"I don't have any . . ." Otto Frank, letter, undated, in the private collection of Buddy Elias.

"I began to read . . ." and "Anne would have so much loved . . ." Otto Frank, memoir.

"But as I grew older . . ." Quoted in Gilbert, *The Boys: The Story of 732 Young Concentration Camp Survivors*, p. 406.

"When I look . . ." Quoted in Gilbert, *The Boys*, pp. 427–28.

"I went to the bunk . . ." and "To the people who say . . ." Quoted in Brown, Stephens, and Rubin, *Images from the Holocaust*, pp. 522–23.

"Will I ever . . ." *The Diary of Anne Frank*, April 5, 1944.

"The most important source . . ." "the most widely read . . ." and "one of the key . . ." Evans and Lunn, *War and Memory in the Twentieth Century*, pp. 3–16.

"I want to go on living . . ." *The Diary of Anne Frank*, April 5, 1944.

BIBLIOGRAPHY
AND FURTHER READING

Anne Frank-Fonds, Basel, Switzerland. Archives.

Anne Frank Magazine 1998. Interview with Miep Gies. Amsterdam: Anne Frank Stichting, 1998.

Anne Frank Stichting, Amsterdam, Holland. Archives.

Anne Frank Stichting. *Anne Frank: A History for Today*, international travelling exhibit, 1996.

Anne Frank Stichting. *Anne Frank: A History for Today*, exhibit catalog. Amsterdam: Anne Frank Stichting, 1996.

Anne Frank Stichting. *Anne aus Frankfurt*, international travelling exhibit, 1990.

Anne Frank Stichting. *Anne Frank in the World: 1929–1945*. New York: Knopf Books for Young Readers, 2001.

Berenbaum, Michael. *The World Must Know: The History of The Holocaust as Told in the United States Holocaust Memorial Museum*. Second edition. Baltimore: Johns Hopkins University Press, 2006.

Brilleslijper, Lientje. Memoir included in film booklet for *Ein Tagebuch für Anne Frank*, VEB Progress Film-Vertrieb, 1959.

Brown, Jean E., Elaine C. Stephens, and Janet E. Rubin, editors. *Images from the Holocaust: A Literature Anthology*. Chicago: NTC/ Contemporary Publishing Group, 1996.

Cohn, Vera. "The Day I Met Anne Frank." *Anti-Defamation League Bulletin*, vol. 13, no. 6 (June 1956).

Dawidowicz, Lucy S. *The War Against the Jews: 1933–1945*. New York: Bantam Books, 1976.

Elias, Buddy, author interview, Cheltenham, October 1997.

Evans, Martin, and Kenneth Lunn, editors. *War and Memory in the Twentieth Century*. Oxford: Berg Publishers, 1997.

Frank, Anne. *The Diary of Anne Frank: The Critical Edition*. Edited by David Barnouw and Gerrold van der Stroom. London: Viking Books, 1989.

Frank, Anne. Letter reprinted in *Stern* magazine, May 21, 1982.

Frank, Anne. *Tales from the Secret Annex*. London: Penguin, 1988.

Frank, Otto. Memoir. Private collection of Buddy Elias.

Frijda, Jetteke. Author interview, Amsterdam, March 1998.

Fussman, Carl. "The Woman Who Would Have Saved Anne Frank." *Newsday Magazine*, interview with Milly Stanfield, March 16, 1995.

Gies, Miep, with Alison Leslie Gold. *Anne Frank Remembered: The Story of the Women Who Helped Hide the Frank Family.* London: Bantam Press, 1987.

Gilbert, Martin. *The Boys: The Story of 732 Young Concentration Camp Survivors.* New York: Owl Books/Henry Holt, 1997.

Gilbert, Martin. *The Holocaust: The Jewish Tragedy.* London: William Collins, 1986.

Gilbert, Martin. *Never Again: A History of the Holocaust.* New York: HarperCollins, 2000.

Gill, Anton. *An Honourable Defeat.* New York: Henry Holt & Co., 1994.

Gryn, Hugo, with Naomi Gryn. *Chasing Shadows: Memories of a Vanished World.* London: Viking, 2000.

Hödl, Elisabeth. "It Must Never Happen Again." In *Surviving the Fire.* Edited by Lilo Klug. Greensboro, N.C.: Open Hand Publishing, 1989.

Klarsfeld, Serge. *French Children of the Holocaust: A Memorial.* New York: New York University, 1997.

Lambert, Angela. "A Portrait of Anne Frank." *The Independent,* interview with Miep Gies, May 4, 1995.

Lee, Carol Ann. *The Hidden Life of Otto Frank.* New York: William Morrow, 2002.

Lindwer, Willy. *The Last Seven Months of Anne Frank.* New York: Pantheon, 1991.

Marshall, Robert. *In the Sewers of Lvov: A Heroic Story of Survival from the Holocaust*. New York: Scribner, 1991.

Metselaar, Menno, Ruud van der Rol, Dineke Stam, and Hansje Gales Loot, Editors. *Anne Frank House: A Museum with a Story*. Amsterdam: The Anne Frank Stiching, 1999.

Netherlands Institute for War Documentation. Interview with Jan Gies. Archive, date unknown.

Netherlands Institute for War Documentation. Interview with Miep Gies. Archive, date unknown.

Netherlands Institute for War Documentation. Interview with Bep Vokuijl. Archive, date unknown.

Newton, Christopher. "Holocaust Children's Art Collection to Be Shown Outside Prague for First Time," Associated Press Article, February 7, 2000.

Nussbaum, Laureen. "Life and Death." *Sunday Oregonian*, October 4, 1992.

O'Shaughnessy, Lynn, "Global Interest Stuns Pen Pals of Anne Frank," interview with Betty Ann Wagner, *Los Angeles Times*, July 24, 1988.

Pick-Goslar, Hanneli, and Alison Leslie Gold. *Memories of Anne Frank: Reflections of a Childhood Friend*. New York: Scholastic Press, 1997.

Pratt, Jane. "Anne Frank We Remember," interview with Otto Frank. *McCall's* 113 (January 1986).

Presser, Jacob. *Ashes in the Wind: The Destruction of Dutch*

Jewry. London: Souvenir Press, Ltd, 1968.

Rauschning, Hermann. *The Voice of Destruction* (1940). Reprint, Gretna, Louisiana: Pelican Publishing Company, 2003.

Rubin, Susan Goldman. *Searching for Anne Frank: Letters from Amsterdam to Iowa*. New York: Harry N. Abrams, 2003.

Schick, Jean Grossman. *The Story Within Her Story*. Amsterdam, 1954. Unpublished manuscript in the Anne Frank Stichting.

Schloss, Eva [Geiringer]. Author interview. London, January 1998.

Schloss, Eva, with Evelyn Julia Kent. *Eva's Story: A Survivor's Tale by the Step-Sister of Anne Frank*. London: WH Allen, 1988.

Schnabel, Ernst. *The Footsteps of Anne Frank*. London: Longman, 1959.

Schoenberner, Gerhard. *The Yellow Star: The Persecution of the Jews in Europe 1933–1945*. New York: Bantam Books, 1973.

Shapiro, Eda. *The Reminiscences of Victor Kugler, the 'Mr Kraler' of Anne Frank's Diary*. Jerusalem: Yad Vashem Studies XIII, 1979.

Shawn, Karen. *The End of Innocence: Anne Frank and the Holocaust*. New York: International Center for Holocaust Studies, Anti-Defamation League of B'nai B'rith, 1989.

Shepard, Richard F. "Anne Frank Letter to Iowa Pen Pal to Be Sold," interview with Betty Ann Wagner, *New York Times*, July 22, 1988.

Silberberg, Edmond. Telephone interview with author, June 1998.

Simon Wiesenthal Center Collection, Los Angeles, California.

Steen, Jürgen, et al. *Anne aus Frankfurt: Leben und Lebenswelt Anne Franks*. Frankfurt am Main: Historisches Museum Frankfurt am Main, 1990.

Steenmeijer, Anna G., and Otto Frank. *A Tribute to Anne Frank*. New York: Doubleday, 1971.

Turner, Barry. *And the Policeman Smiled: 10,000 Children Escape from Nazi Europe*. London: Bloomsbury, 1991.

van Last Galen, Dick, and Rolf Wolfswinkel. *Anne Frank and After: Dutch Holocaust Literature in Perspective*. Amsterdam: Amsterdam University Press, 1996.

van Maarsen, Jacqueline, retold for children by Carol Ann Lee. *A Friend Called Anne*. New York: Viking, 2005.

van Maarsen, Jacqueline. *My Friend Anne Frank*. New York: Vantage Press, 1996.

van Maarsen, Jacqueline. Author interviews. London, January 1998; Amsterdam, February 1998.

You Magazine—The Mail on Sunday. "I Knew the Real Anne Frank." Interview with Buddy Elias. February 2, 1997.

Zapruder, Alexandra. *Salvaged Pages: Young Writers' Diaries of the Holocaust*. New Haven, Conn.: Yale University Press, 2002.

TEXT PERMISSIONS